Cornelia Parker Never Endings

Cornelia Parker Never Endings

IKON

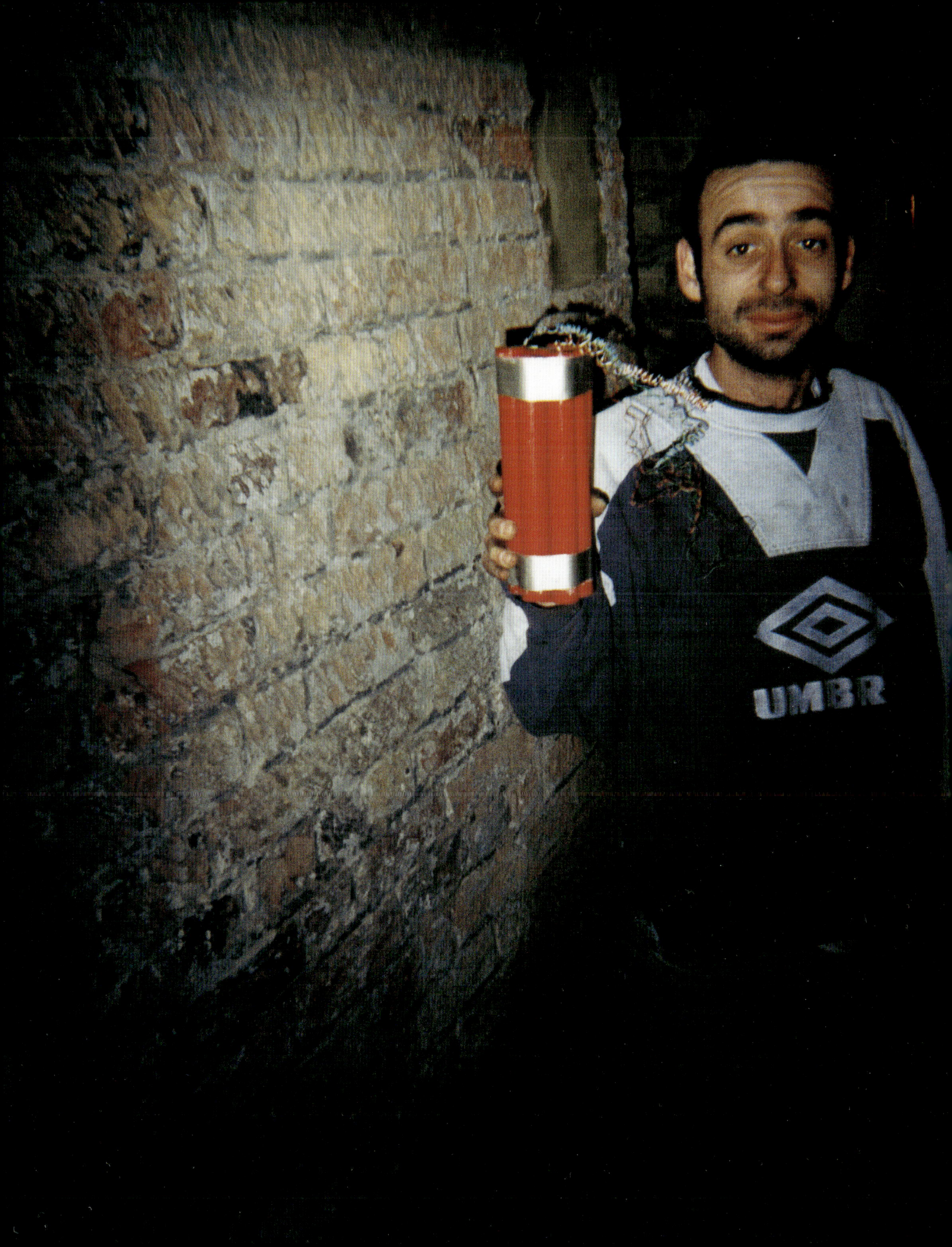
UMBR

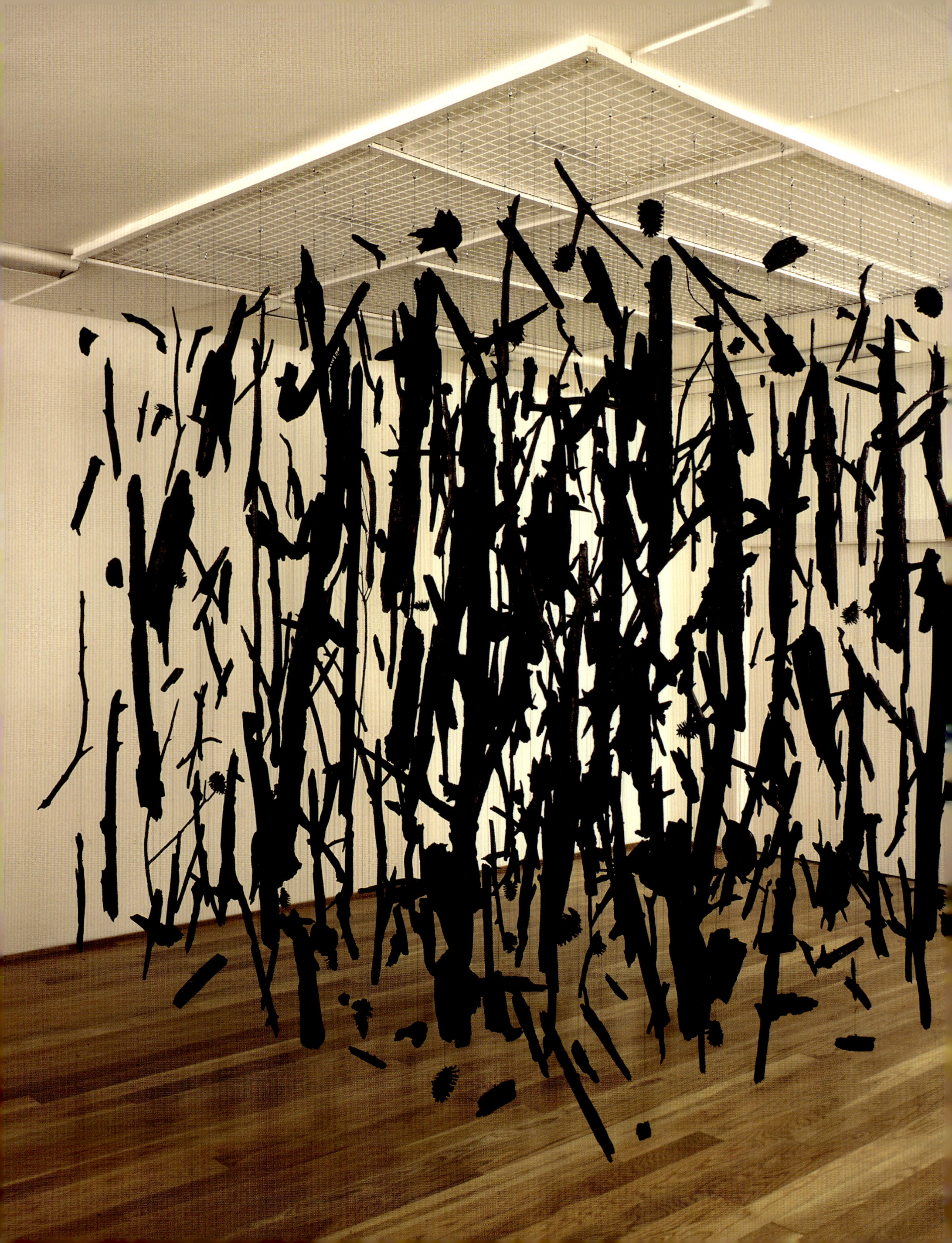

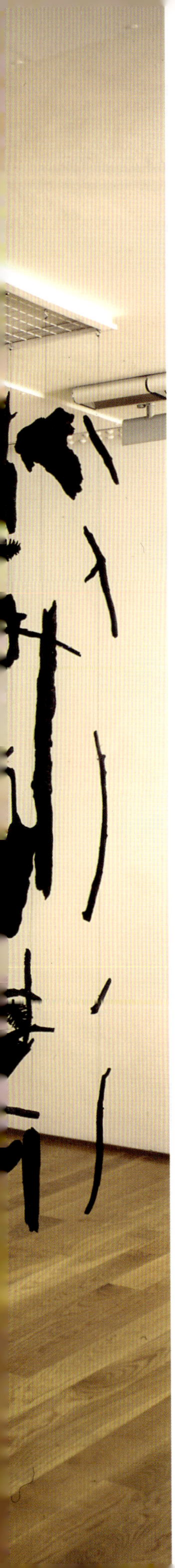

Heart of Darkness 2004

Foreword

This is the first survey of new and recent work by Cornelia Parker in the UK for ten years. Characteristically ambitious in both form and content, it involves a wide range of media; sculptural pieces, incorporating readymades, photography, recorded sound, and video. Such variety belies a remarkably consistent fundamental proposition, at once testing and positive, marking out the artist above all for her aesthetic and philosophical integrity.

Heart of Darkness, one of the most visually striking works here, is an installation comprising remnants of a devastating forest fire that happened in Florida in 2004. Started by the US Forestry Department as a routine "controlled burn", fuelled by high winds, it quickly began to rage out of control, to the extent that the resulting wildfire now has a place in popular memory as the "Impassable One". Parker recreates a section of the forest using the burnt bits of timber suspended from the ceiling of a high white room, an extraordinary three-dimensional charcoal drawing. The work is a resurrection, formalising fragments of a destructive event. An anti-monument to human interaction with nature, it arises from an artistic strategy very familiar within the context of Parker's work overall.

The sublime nature of terrestrial and cosmic phenomena has inspired this artist's practice from the first. *Killing Time* uses filmed footage she took on four consecutive days at an unspecified location in the American landscape. We witness a group of tourists waiting, watching with cameras ready to capture a breathtaking event. They are expectant in this situation, full of anticipation, talking about something they're sure is imminent, and thus Parker alludes to all sorts of things we might be waiting for – even the end of the world.

Environmental disaster is something that concerns this artist now more than ever. Interestingly it represents the inversion of a previous theme, whereby humankind is subject to unstoppable natural forces; now there is the idea of the world, due to human agency, slipping towards what Parker refers to as a "quieter apocalypse … [the] chance that the planet may not be able to sustain human life by the end of this century". It was this that prompted Parker to request an interview with Noam Chomsky, the acclaimed philosopher whose grasp of world politics is as challenging as it is profoundly reasonable. In the resulting video, *Chomskian Abstract*, he dwells on this worrying moment in history when America and other world powers seem paralysed in the face of self-inflicted catastrophe.

It is typical of Cornelia Parker that she would seek out Chomsky. She is an artist that grapples with difficult problems, often engaging with subjects that loom large in popular imagination, universal triggers perhaps of a collective unconscious. Here also is the actual nightgown worn by Mia Farrow in *Rosemary's Baby*; here, clods of earth from underneath the Leaning Tower of Pisa; here, the sound recordings of spiritual mediums affected by the psychic energy permeating the home of Charlotte Brontë; here, a doll cut in half by the guillotine that beheaded Marie Antoinette.

Cornelia Parker's work is remarkable for its uncompromising quality. On the other hand, it could not be more open, both in terms of the meanings of finished pieces and the processes involved. Concerning the latter, many individuals and organisations have collaborated with us towards the realisation of this exhibition. Norman Cherry and Terry Hunt at the Birmingham School of Jewellery, Roger Hancox and Bill Harding at the Gun Barrel Proof House, Andrew McCarthy at the Brontë Parsonage Museum and Dr Andrew Wilson at the Department of Archaelogy, Bradford University gave invaluable help and advice. The Henry Moore Foundation and The Sharjah Biennial also have been very generous. Thanks to all at Frith Street Gallery and D'Amelio Terras, and also to those who have lent us work, thereby giving this project other strong dimensions. We are extremely grateful to Jane Hamlyn, John Smith, Mike Perry, Sue Jones and Jeff McMillan for both practical and moral support. Finally, thanks to Cornelia Parker for her unique genius.

Jonathan Watkins
Director

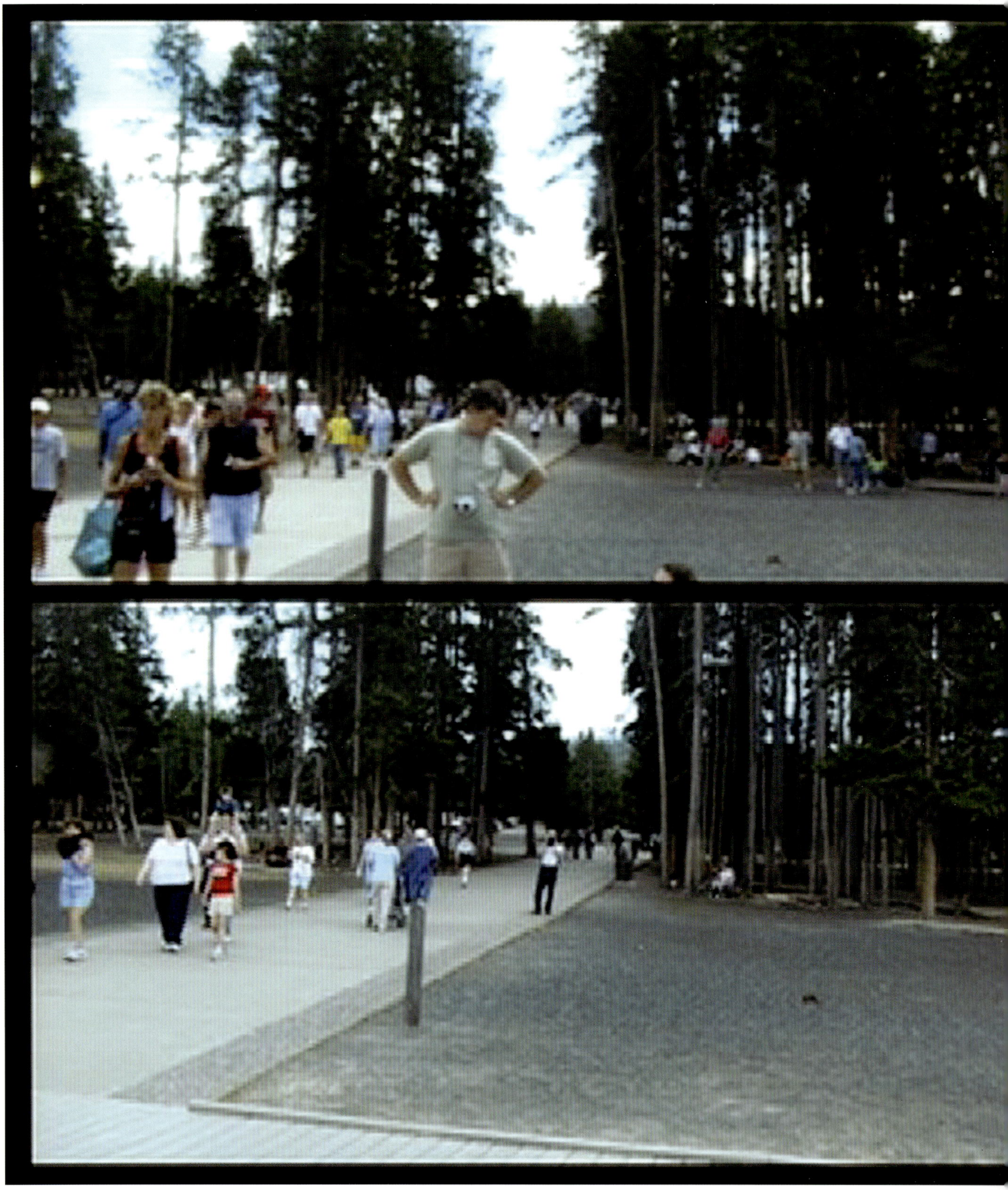

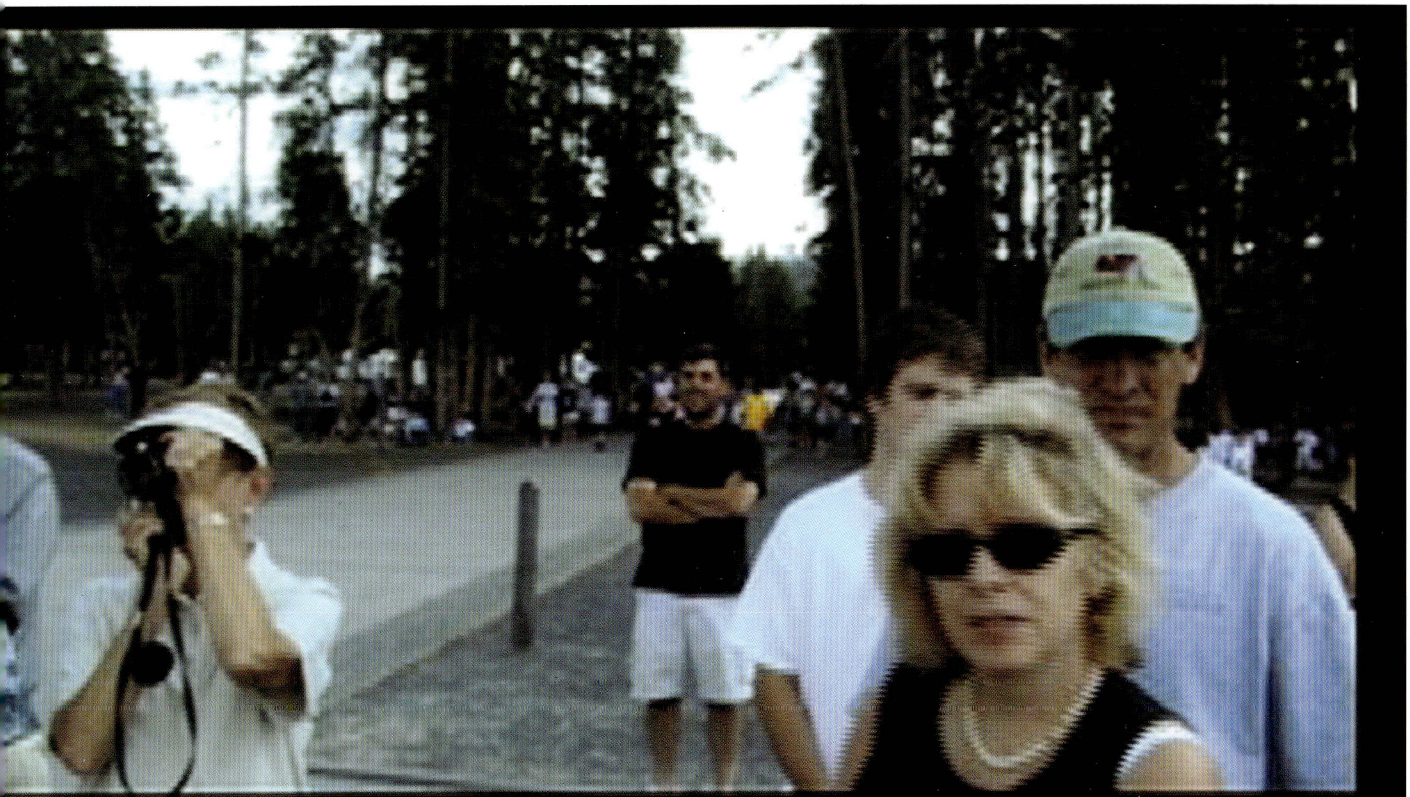

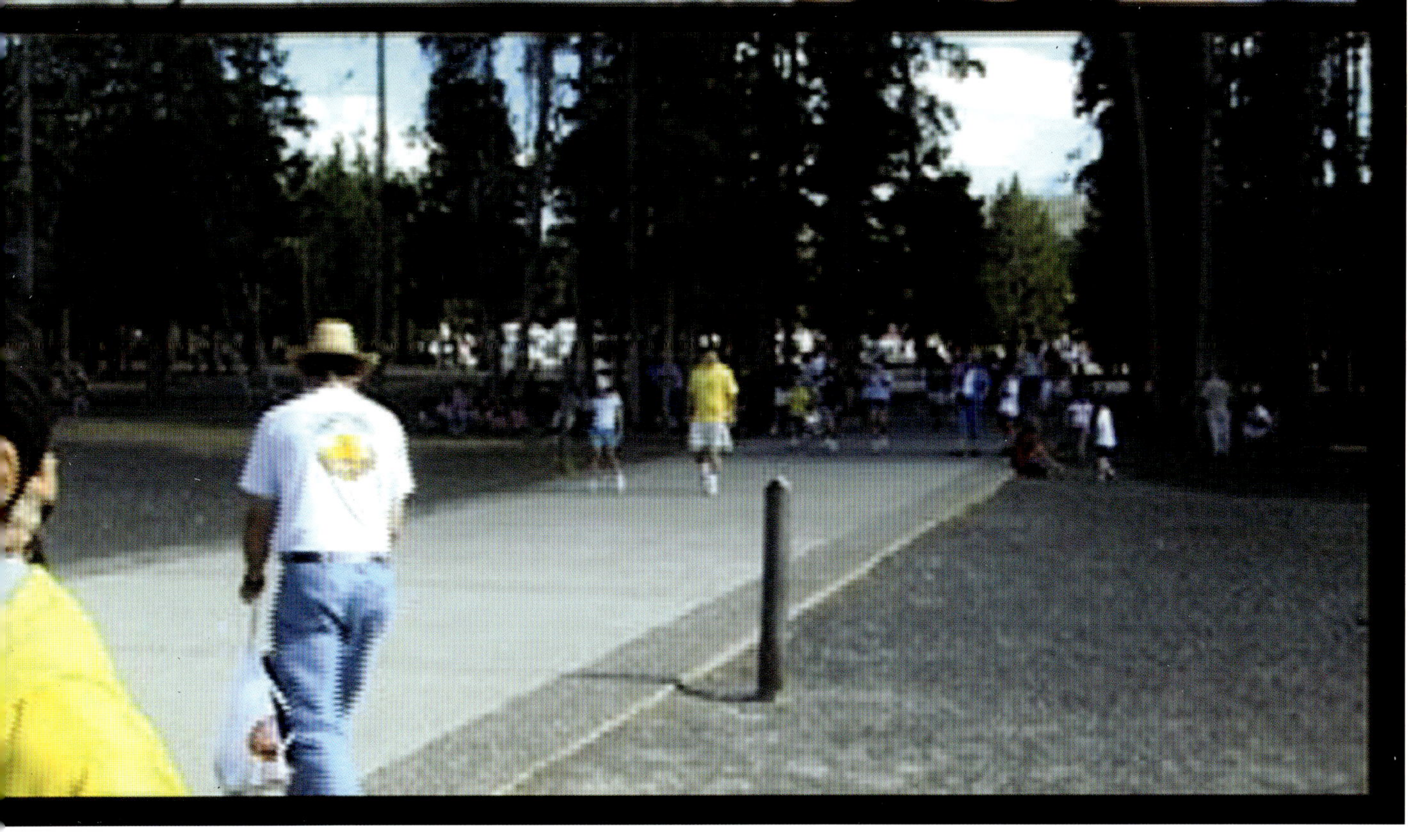

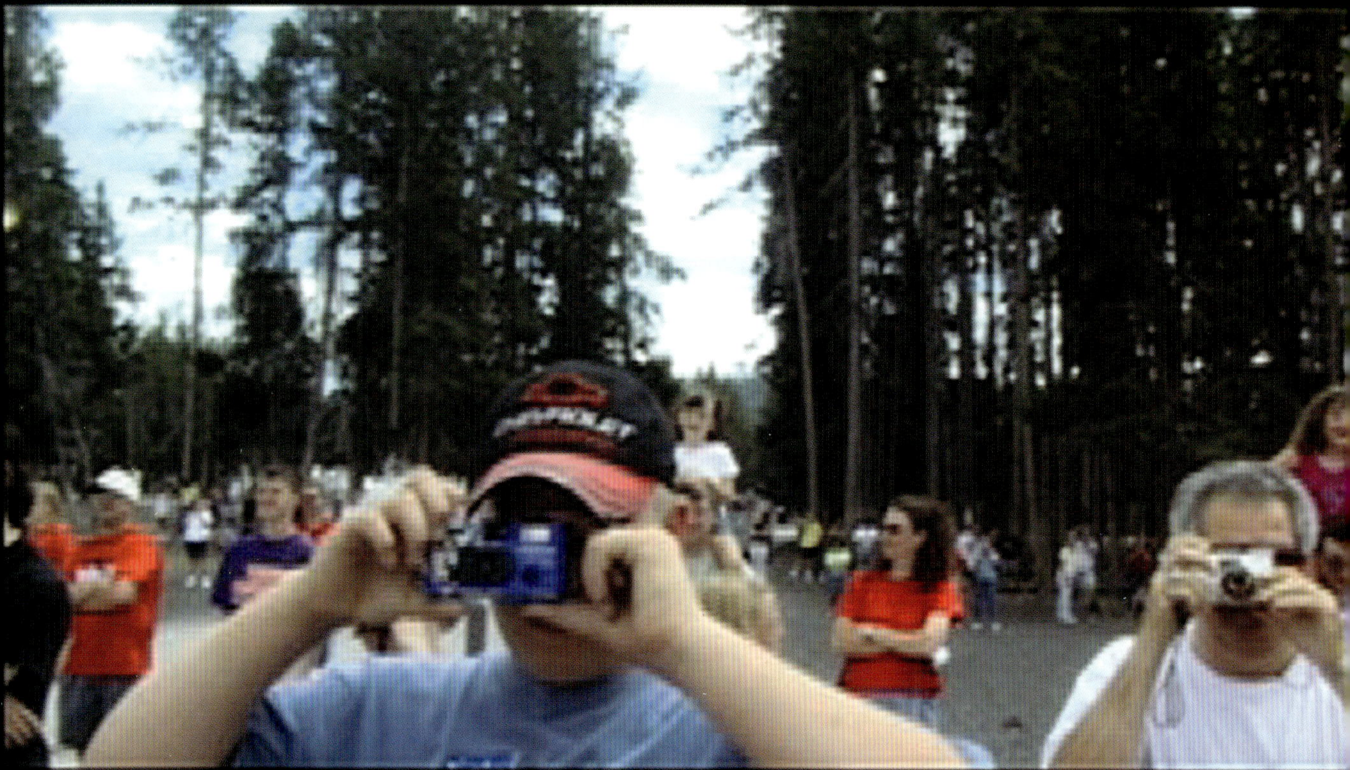

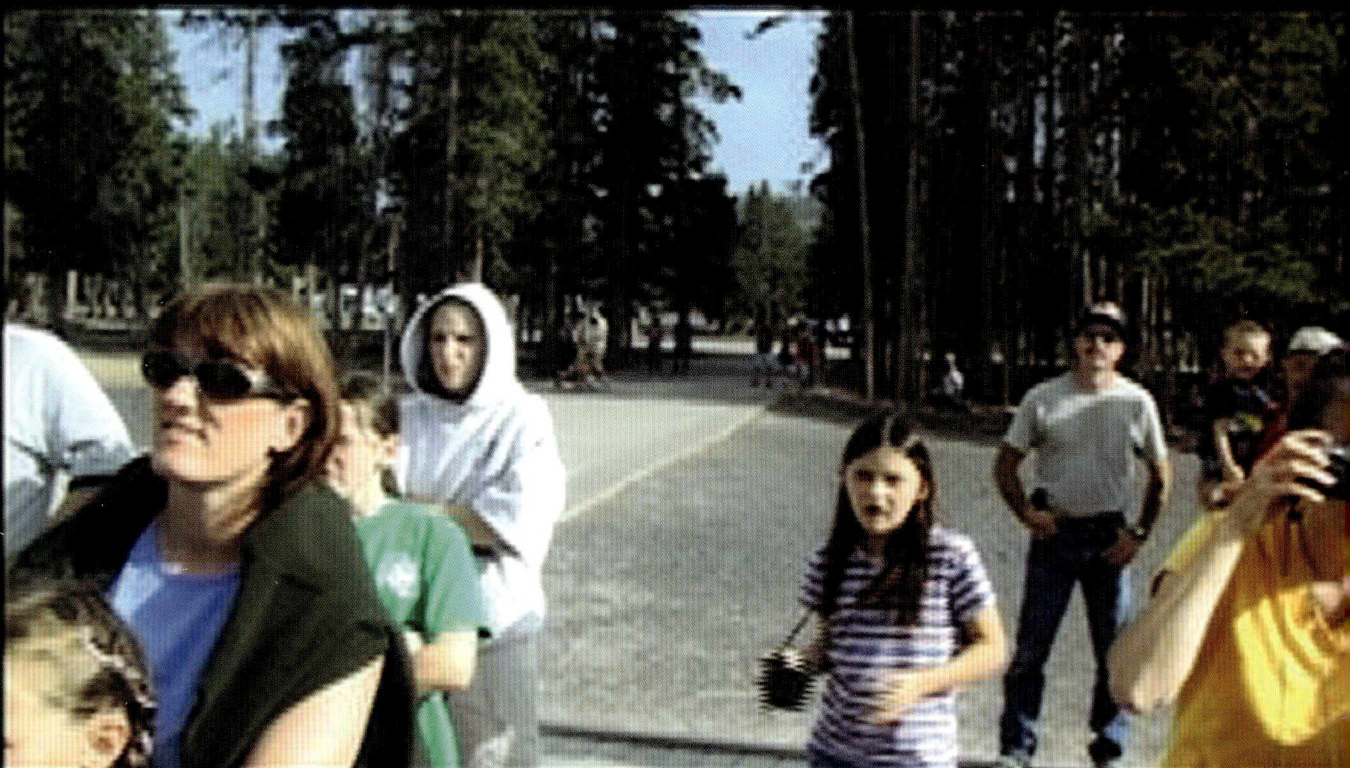

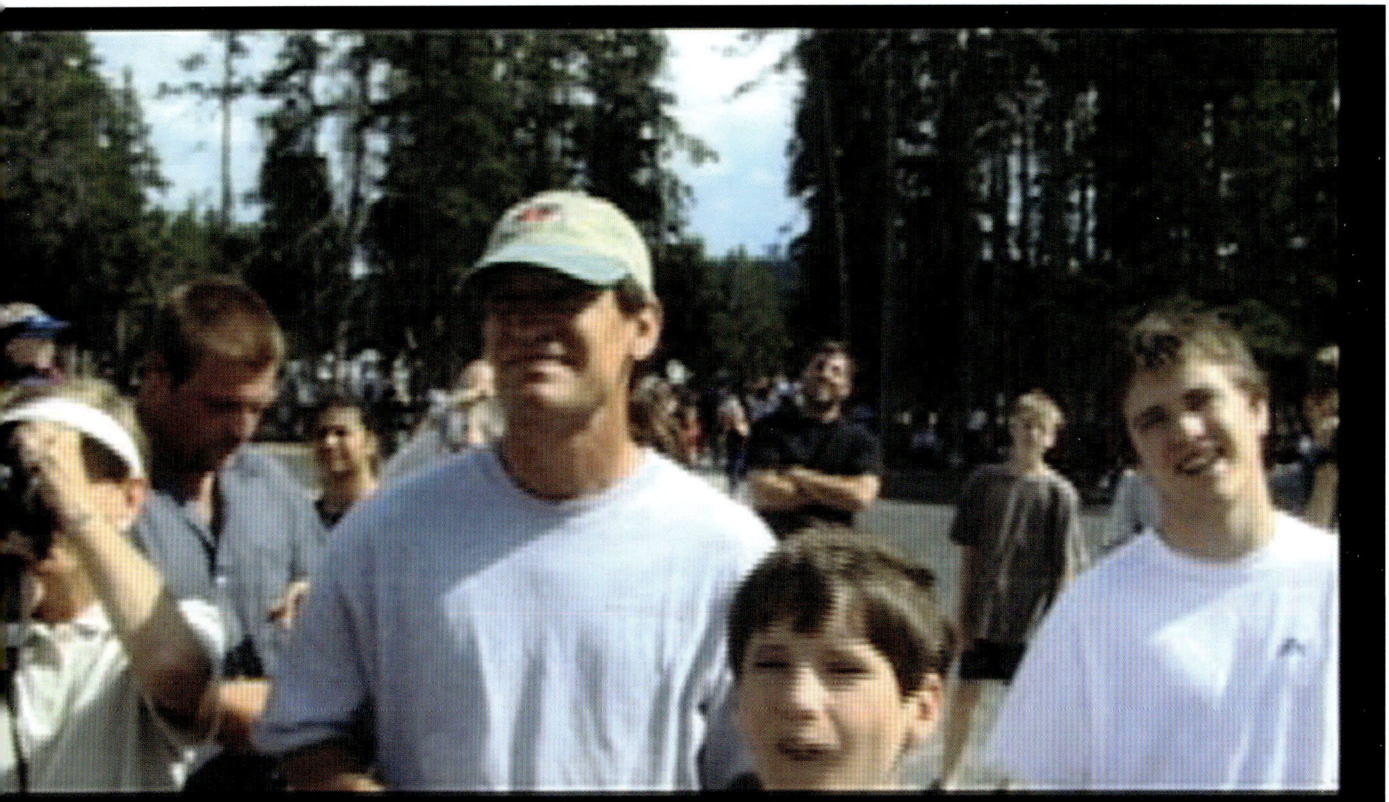

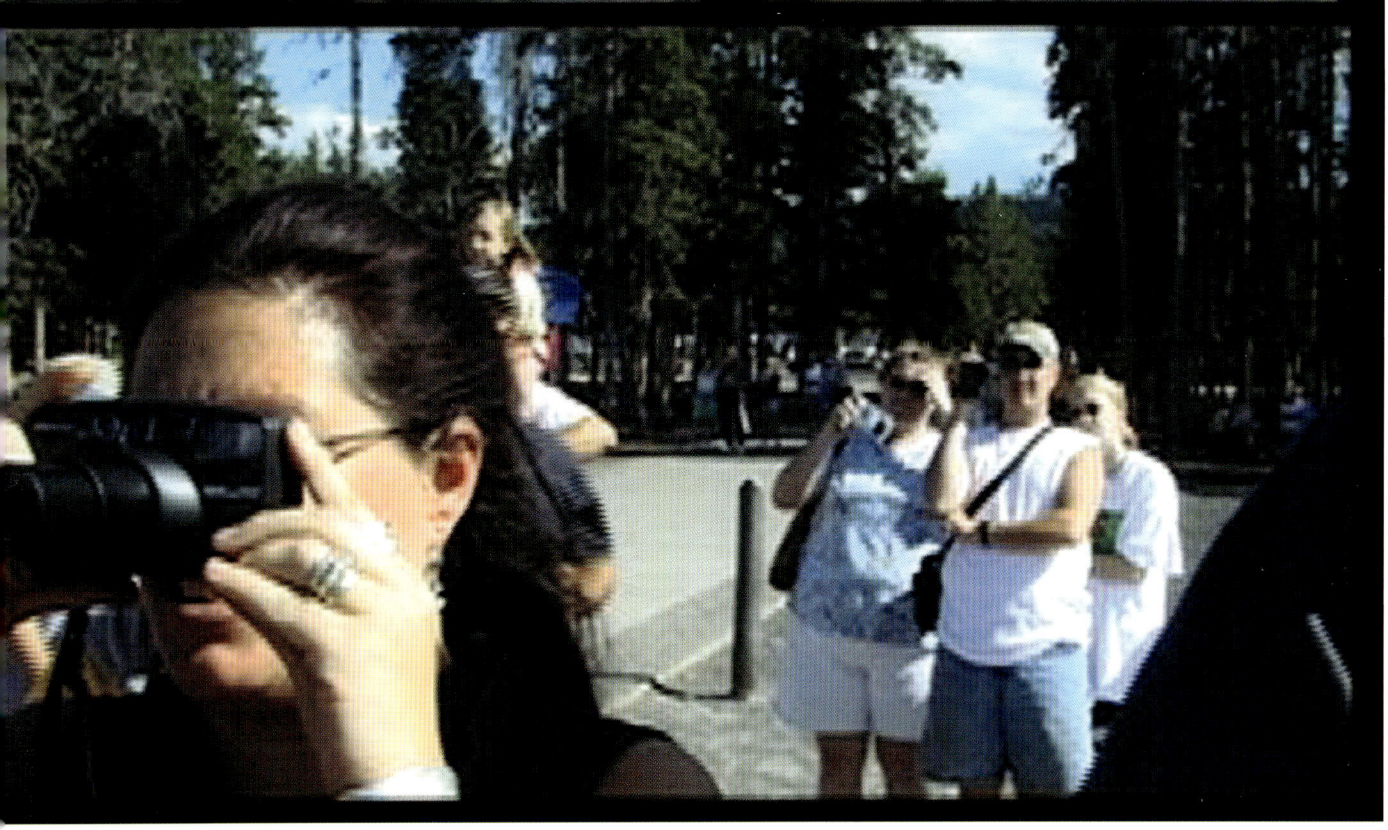

Wires and Other Drawings

Cameras poised, watches checked, the sun-drenched tourists in *Killing Time* are waiting to witness some event. We watch them gather, take their photographs, and finally we see them drift away, slightly disappointed, but perhaps relieved that one of the things they simply had to see is now behind them, and has been seen.

What we don't see is the centre of attraction, the spectacle itself. Something has drawn their attention, but we are drawn purely to them.

The ability to miss the point, escape the thing, and attend to the connections and the in-betweens lies at the heart of drawings of many different kinds. It's a simple trick, but a powerful one: don't focus on the coastlines, but the edges of the seas; don't look at the trees, but the shapes between the leaves. And to do as Cornelia Parker does, and go on to turn these negative spaces into rich, full positives, is to work a rare kind of magic on things. Background noise is brought to the fore; undersides are flipped onto surfaces; the ephemeral is given centre-stage: *Blue Shift* brings us the light without the source, the trappings of celebrity without the star. Off-cuts, scraps, and residues are rendered more important than their origins: *Stolen Thunder* puts the silverware aside and offers us the tarnish in its stead.

Parker does not simply want to show us things in a different light: her aim is less to perform an intellectual deconstruction of the real, than to flatten it, explode it, shoot at it, steamroller it, interrupt it, mangle it, boil it down, take some kind of sledgehammer to it and see what comes out of the crisis she provokes, what emerges on the other side. Her interest is in undoing things, rearranging them, and placing them, mutated, in the gallery. She doesn't represent things, but interrupts processes and alters states: *Embryo Firearms* arrests the development of Colt 45s just before they have a chance to become guns. She pulls metals into wires, stretching objects into threads and giving them new narratives, new lifelines: *Pulled Tooth Drawing* draws dental gold; *Bullet Drawings* draw lead bullets. Sometimes these threads are lines of measurement: a silver dollar drawn out to the height of the Statue of Liberty; a war medal drawn to the 'measure' of a man.

Much of Parker's work involves experiments, and what we see are her results: not the proven findings of scientific research, but what turns out to be the case, what is left, what remains. *Endless Column III* suspends silver-plated objects, which have been crushed in a

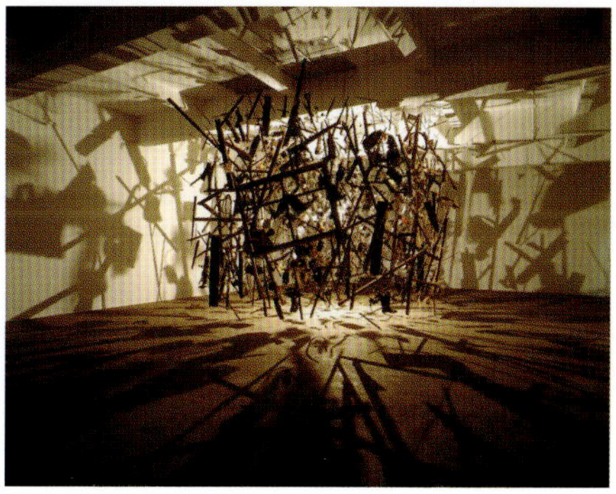

Cold Dark Matter: An Exploded View 1991

250 ton industrial press. In 1991 she famously engaged British Army personnel to blow up a carefully assembled garden shed, suspending the remnants to make one of her most celebrated works, *Cold Dark Matter: An Exploded View*.

Parker doesn't always orchestrate events: *Subconscious of a Monument* suspends clods of earth removed from beneath the Leaning Tower of Pisa in an effort to stop it leaning too far; *Shadow of a Doubt* suspends wood reclaimed from a ghost town in Texas so that it appears to recline against the gallery wall. *Heart of Darkness* strings up pieces of charcoal taken from the aftermath of a wildfire in Florida. These works are less found objects than found events.

But whether they are found or made, and however they are hung, Parker's mutations of things are events in the life of matter which draw our attention to both its mutability and also the constraints within which it can be changed: "you can only make things do what's physically possible for them to do," Parker once said in an interview, "however much you try to control them." These are the words of an artisan, in the highest sense of the word: one who knows how to collaborate with her materials, rather than trying to impose on them; one who is willing to allow them to explore and express themselves.

Little of the structure and substance of things can be perceived with the naked eye. And while she works close to her materials, Parker's close-up photographs and microscopic images betray a longing to get closer still. Her forensic interest in the stuff of the Brontës' lives – the pen-nibs, inks, and papers, the artefacts and accessories after the facts of their work – implies a kind of animistic faith that things can be loaded with less tangible details too. Histories and memories attach themselves to the apparently inanimate; objects have dream lives, a subconscious of their own which might be discernible if only we knew how to tune into it. This desire to divine the imperceptible is, of course, insatiable: no matter how high the resolution, however clear the images, there is always a scale still smaller, a register still higher, a level of detail more refined. The heart of things will always evade scrutiny.

Still, great treasures can be found along the way. Counting its magnifications in the hundreds, rather than the tens of conventional microscopes, the electron microscope reveals a

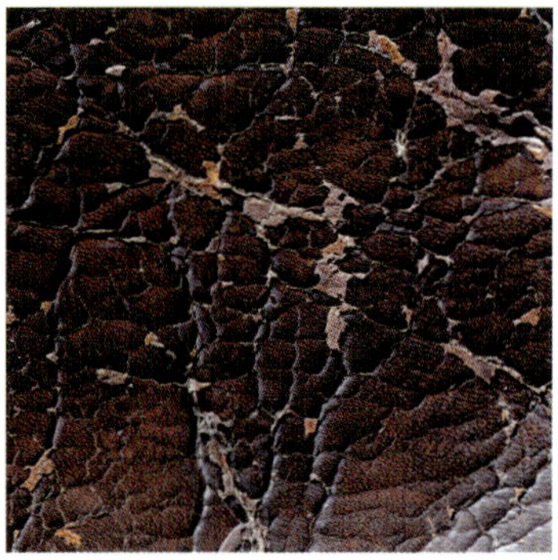

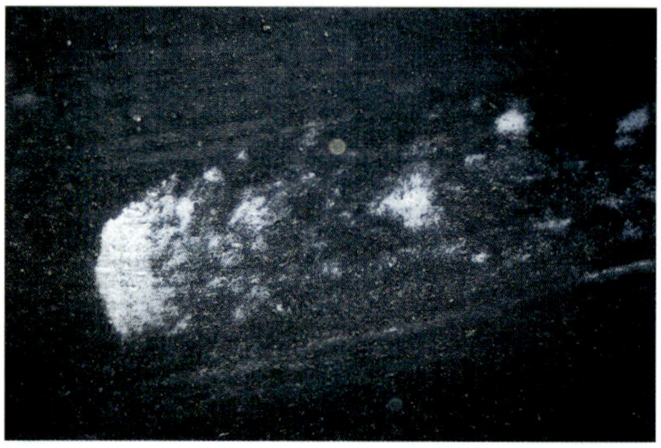

left
Marks made by Freud, Subconsciously 2000

right
Einstein Abstracts 1999
(detail)

molecular reality of unimaginable complexity. The images it makes are astounding, but it is not an optical device: rather than gazing at objects, it can be said to touch their surfaces, feeling its way across their contours as though with electronic fingertips. Its processes are tactile, not visible: only later does it offer us its findings in a form that we can process with our eyes. What we see are the after-images of a touching encounter with materiality.

Further still inside the workings of the world are fields and forces of magnitudes and complexities we can barely begin to comprehend. These are the webs of influence in which Parker's suspended works are caught. Today's physicists talk in terms of strings, superstrings and sheets of space-time continuity; Einstein dreamed of discovering waves in the fabric of space-time which would explain the workings of gravity. But this most basic influence, the very thing that keeps us down to earth, remains a fascinating mystery. We know where we would be without it: were its forces to be weaker, we would float away; just a little stronger and we'd sink into the ground. Gravity holds things together and keeps them apart just enough to make them possible.

Parker's magnificent suspensions take this sense of perfect poise just a little further, so that we can see just how precariously we too are compelled to hang around the surface of the earth, only slightly lower than the artefacts she hangs, not too high and not too low, not too dense or scattered, not too solid or too loose.

Objects do not live, but they are lively, and far more influential on our thinking than has been traditionally supposed. If things can be invested with histories of their own, so too can they affect the world of narratives, ideas, the theories and the workings of the minds that have so often been prioritised over the messiness of matter itself. For Parker's *Einstein Abstracts*, the chalk marks made by Einstein on the blackboard as he gave a lecture on relativity in Oxford in the 1930s are magnified to the point at which they resemble skids or scudding clouds. In *Freudian Abstracts* she works with the physical materials of Freud's couch; *Marks made by Freud, Subconsciously*, details the creases and rubbings and tears in the leather covering of his chair. This attention to what Freud sat on, rather than what he stood for, wrote down, or spoke about, is not just a witty commentary on his work: it is an endorsement of the importance of material culture as a kind of foundation, a cultural unconscious, the matters underlying our aesthetics and ideas.

For her *Chomskian Abstract*, however, Parker's focus shifts. Now she is studying the contours of a seventy-nine year old face; the relic in this case is a video; the matters in question are those of ecological catastrophe and military might. One of the most powerful themes to emerge from this interview with the American philosopher and commentator Noam Chomsky is the sense of fear, the tension, that has always bubbled under America, keeping it in a state of suspense as it waits for some threat of other to materialise, a limbo which is used to legitimise a heavy-handed state and a war economy. It was the Russians yesterday; today it's the Arabs, tomorrow the Chinese. Any enemy will do, as long as the country's on the edge of its seat.

Chomsky laments the destruction in Iraq, especially that of so many sites of crucial importance to western, and global, history: the looting of the Baghdad Museum, the destruction of so many Sumerian sites, the remains of the ancient city of Babylon, subjected to terrible abuses when the US military established a base on the site just after the invasion in 2003: a brick pavement more than two and a half thousand years old was crushed by military vehicles; thousands of sandbags were filled with earth containing archaeological remains of incalculable value. Worse still is the savage undoing of so much contemporary cultural life: the schools, the universities, the booksellers' markets and the libraries.

Unlike Parker's explosions and shootings, these destructions, with the loss of so much culture and so many lives, cannot be hung in a gallery: this is not a creative unravelling, but the crudest kind of violence, pure brutality, the work of a "barbaric, savage culture", in Noam Chomsky's words.

We draw breath, but not conclusions. One might wish that she had drawn more bullets into wire, taken more guns out of commission, and kept the army occupied with creative destructions like exploding garden sheds. But Parker has taken us on journeys in and out and all around the things we think we know so well, shifting our attention from the world we see to the one she wants us to encounter. Her lines of enquiry are limitless; all her destinations are just pauses on the way. There are never endings in her work.

Sadie Plant

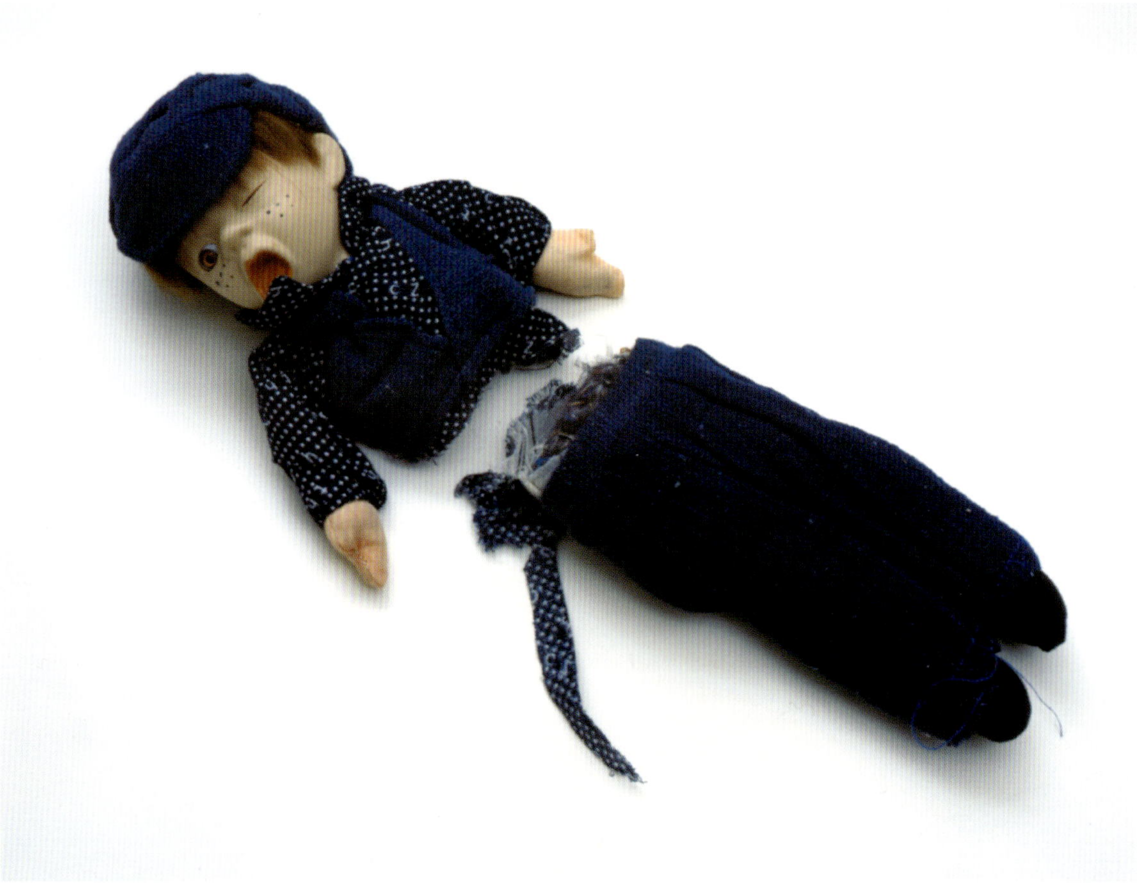

Shared Fate (Oliver) 1998

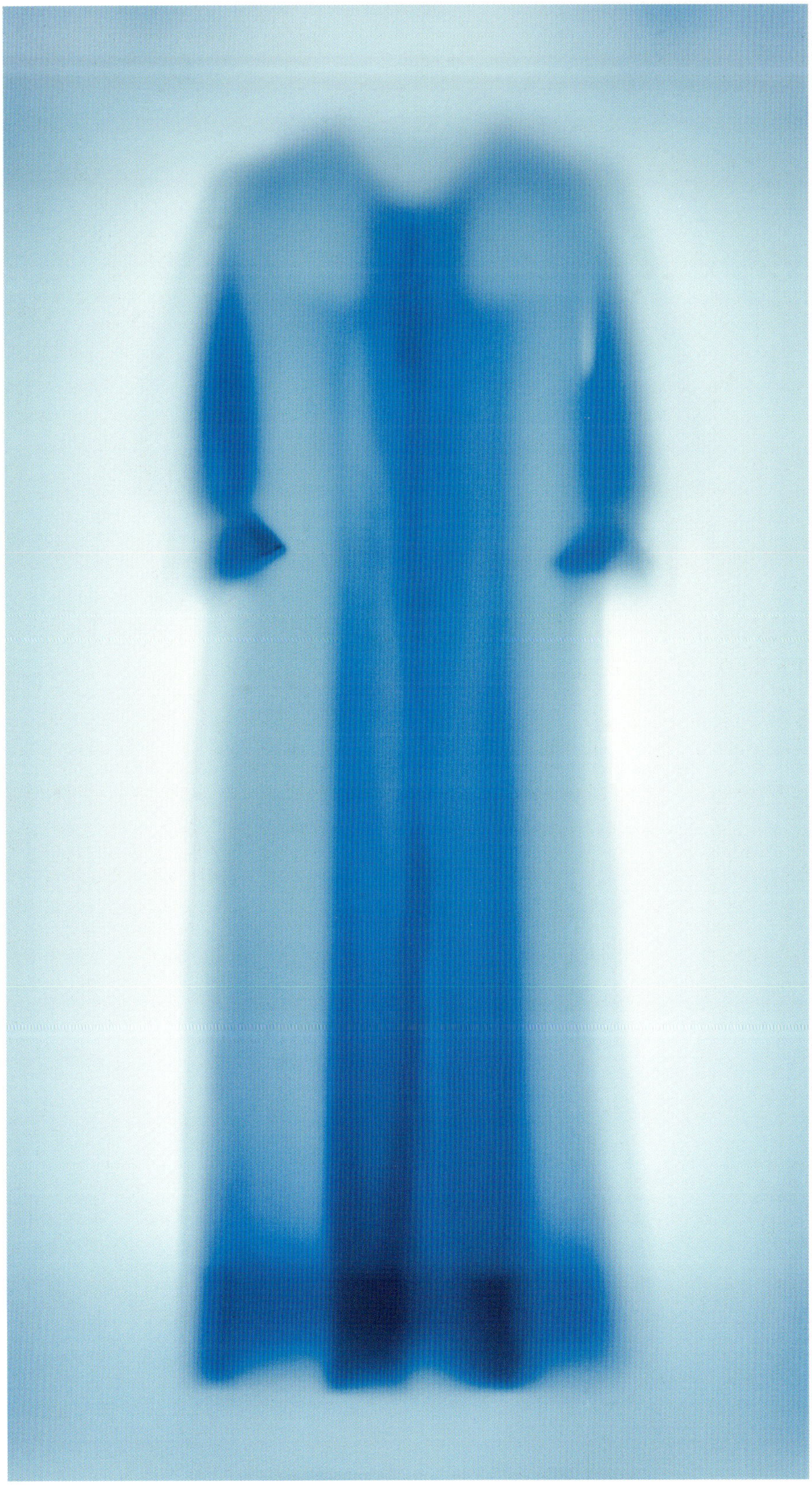

Blue Shift 2001

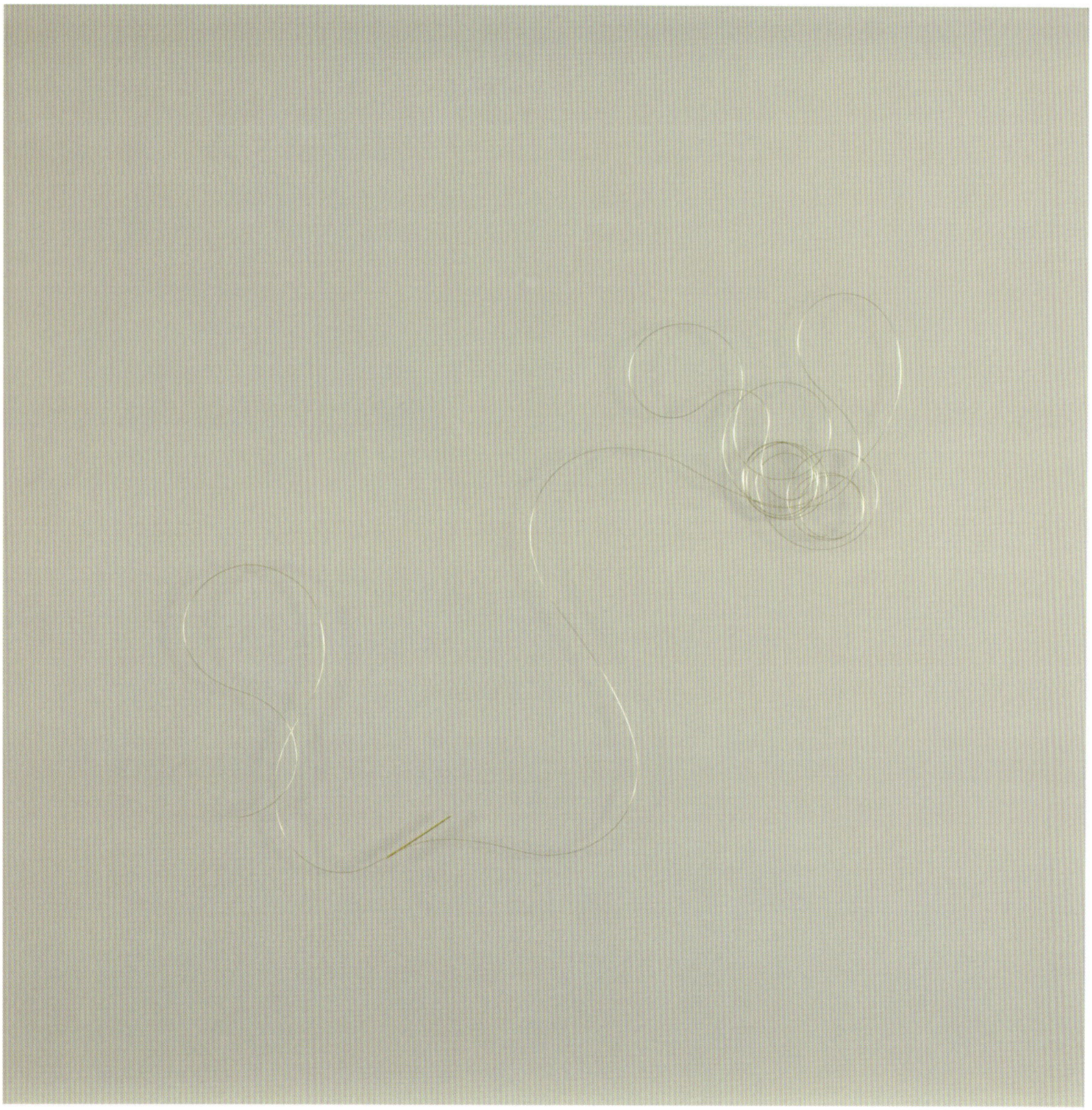

Pulled Tooth Drawing 2007

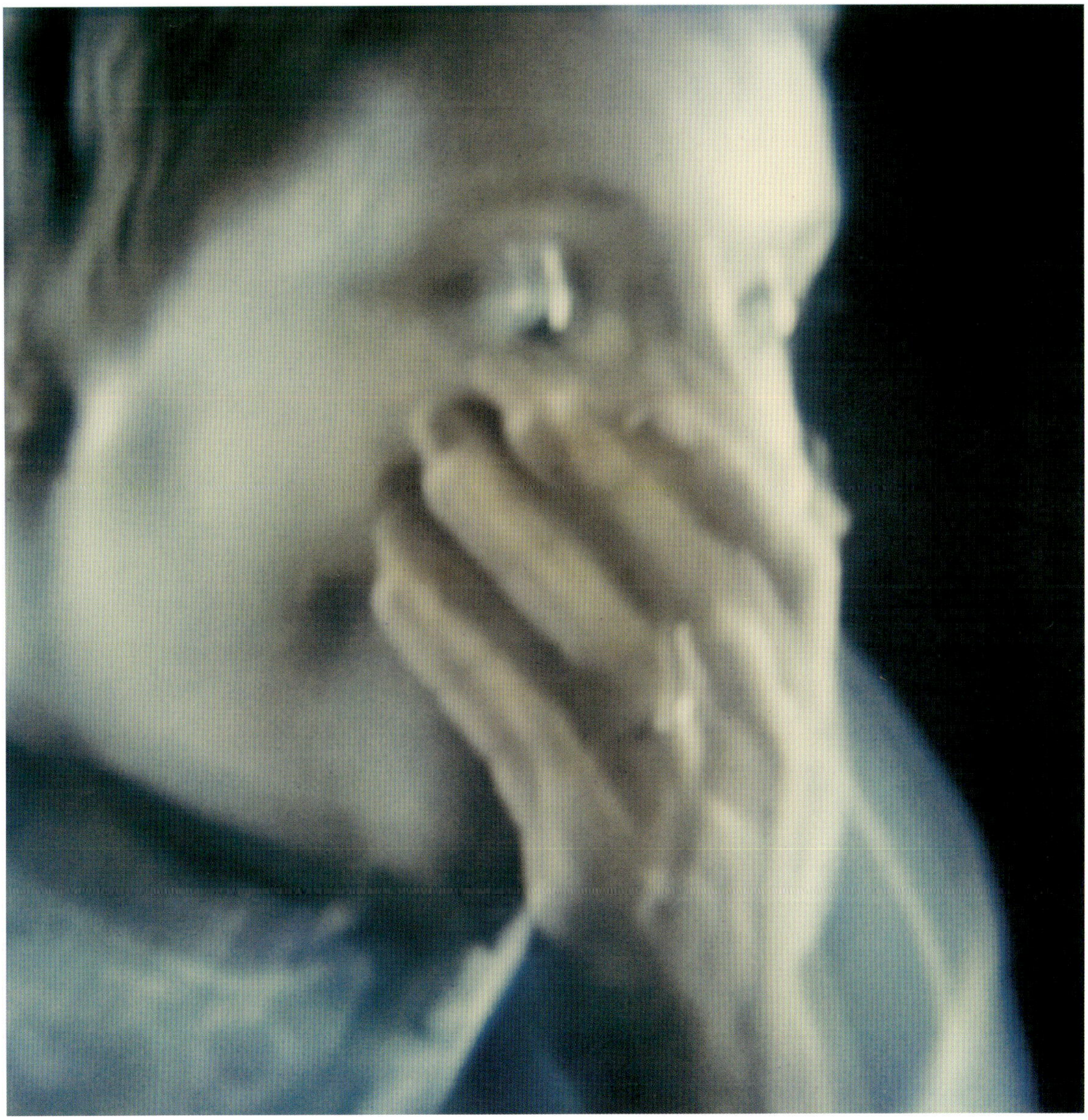

Blue Shift 2002

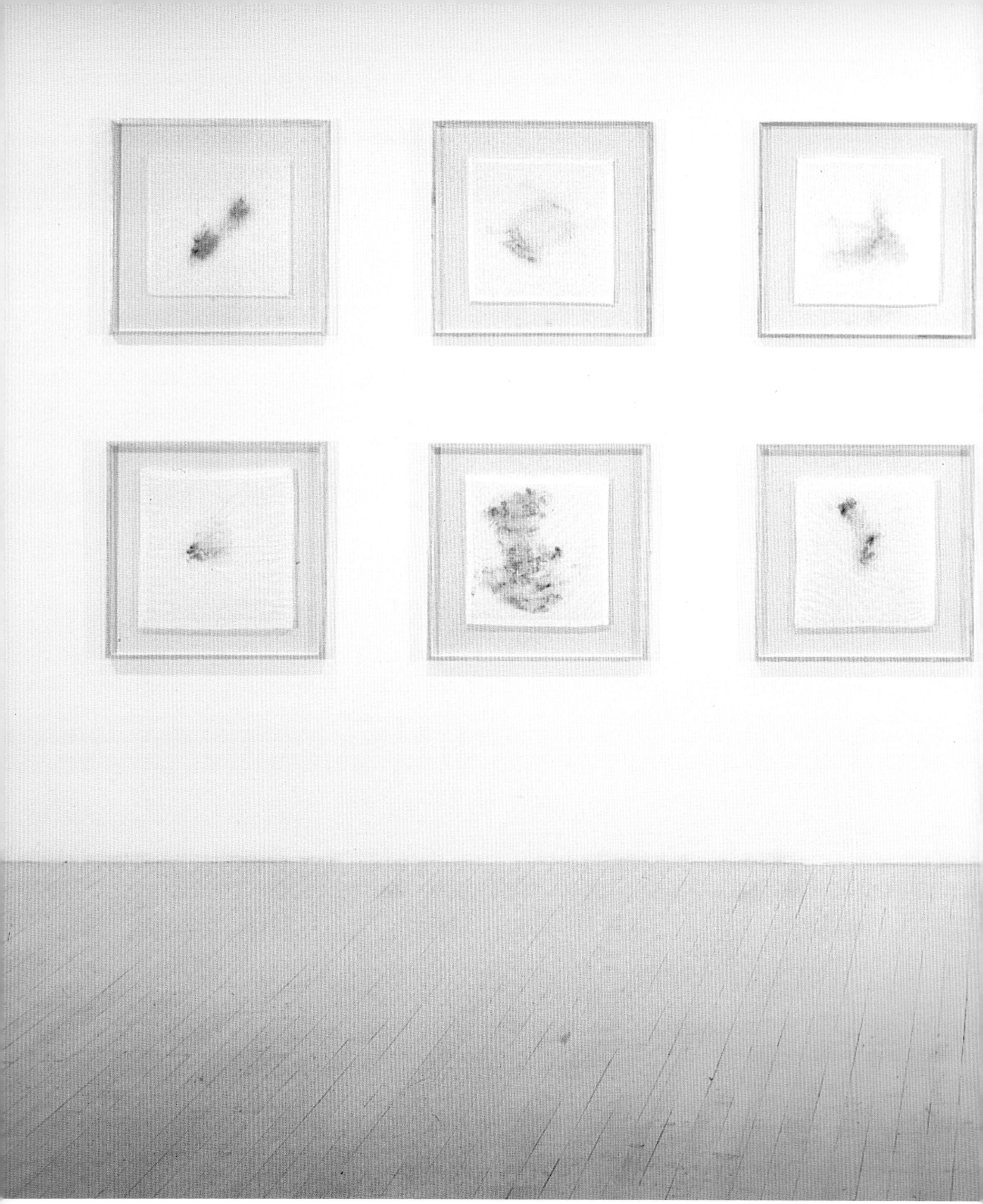

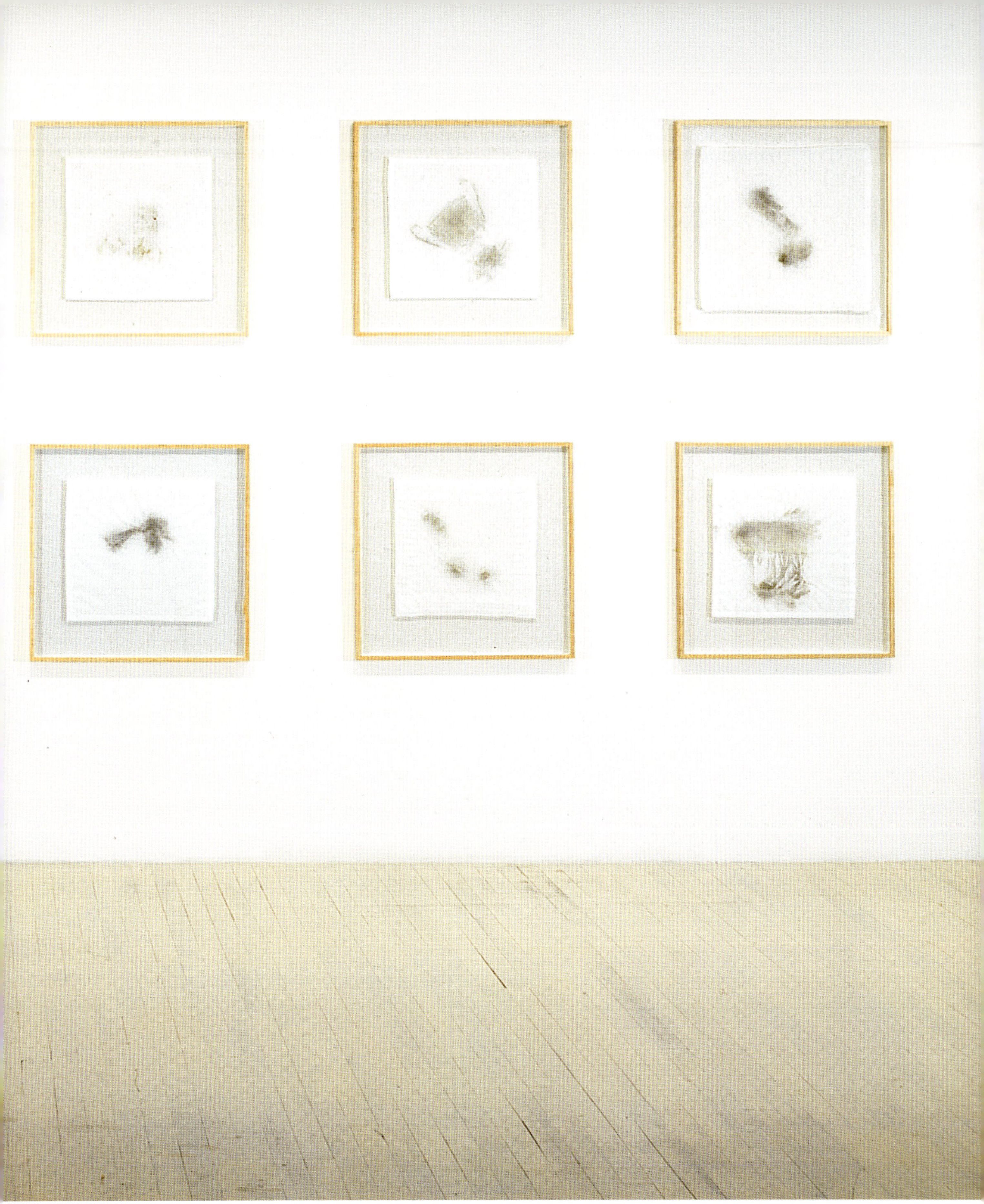

Stolen Thunder 1997–98

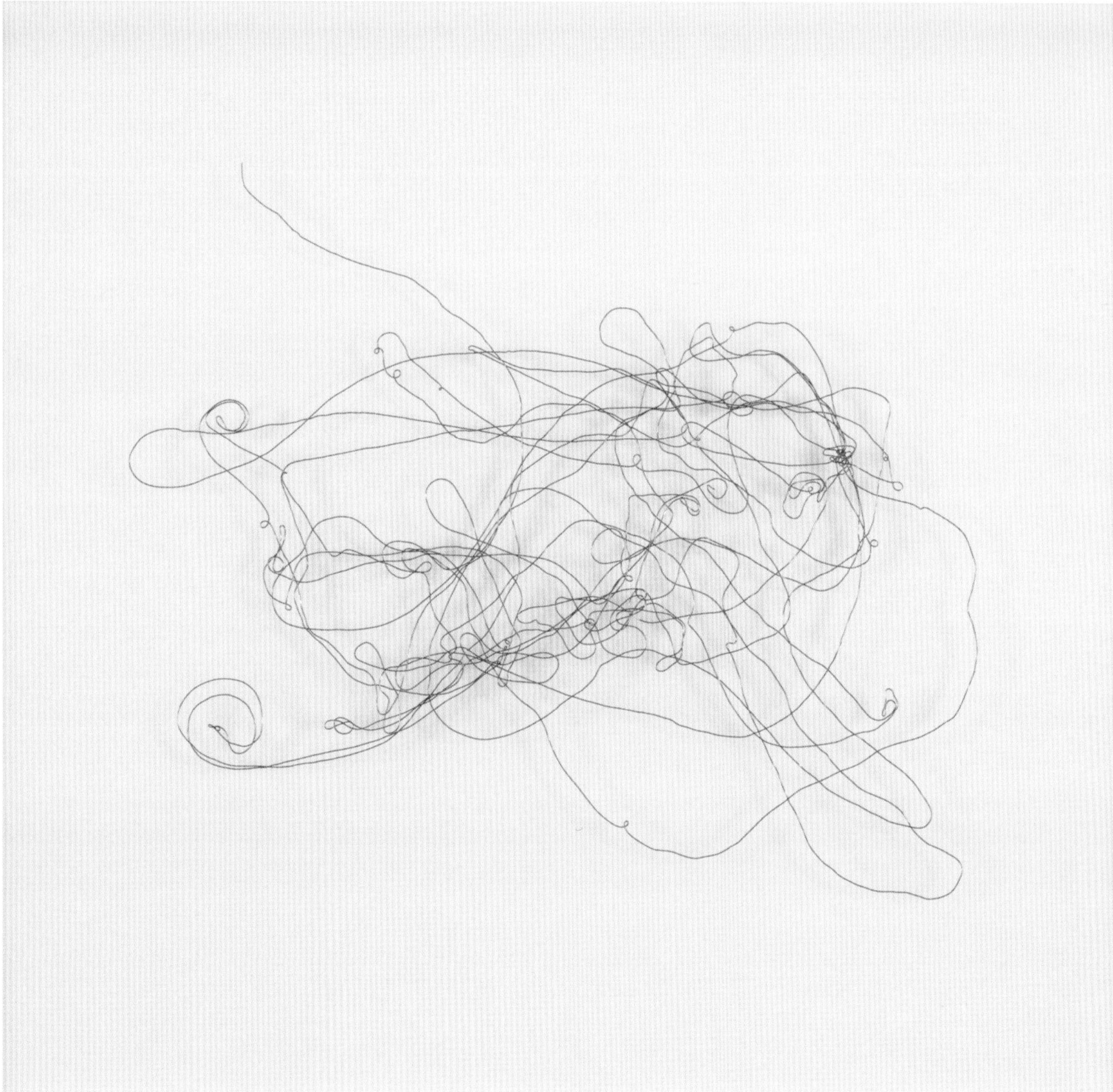

 Bullet Drawing 2007

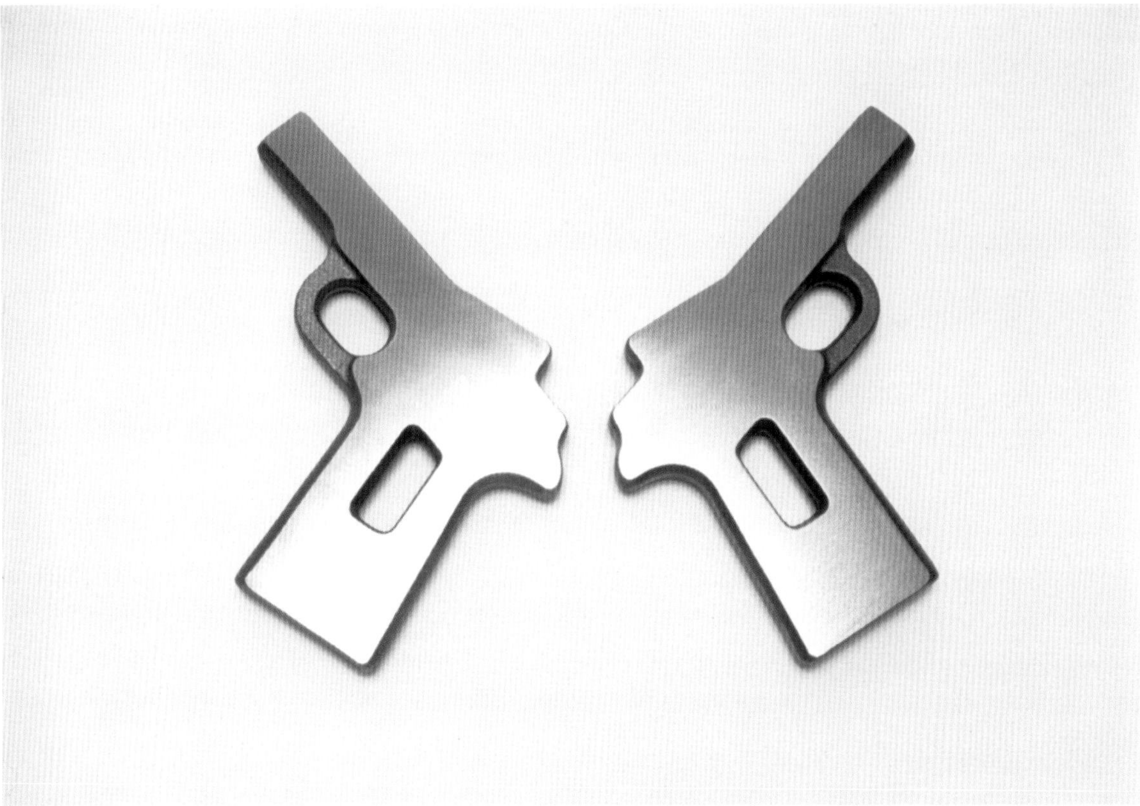

Embryo Firearms 1995

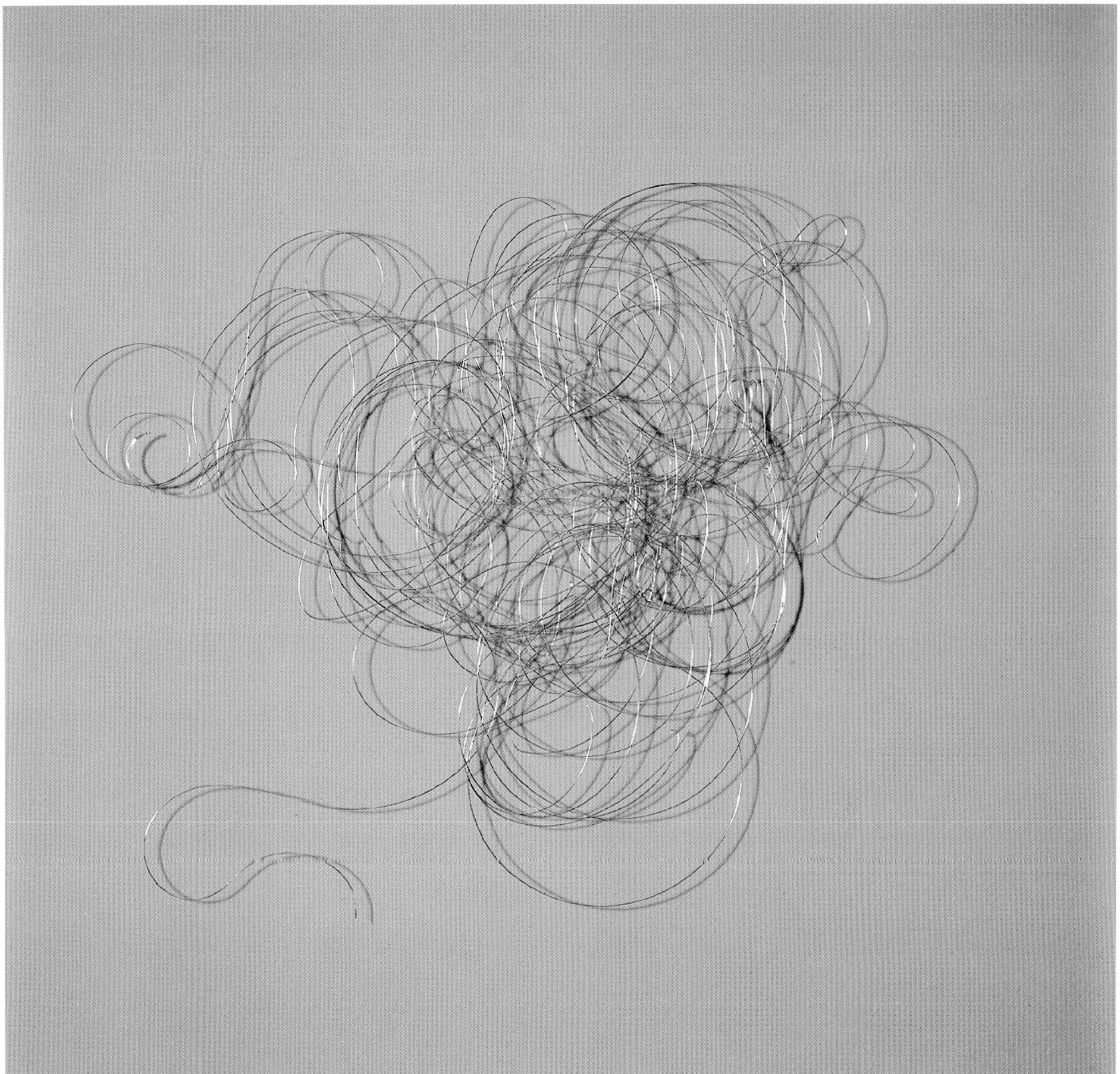

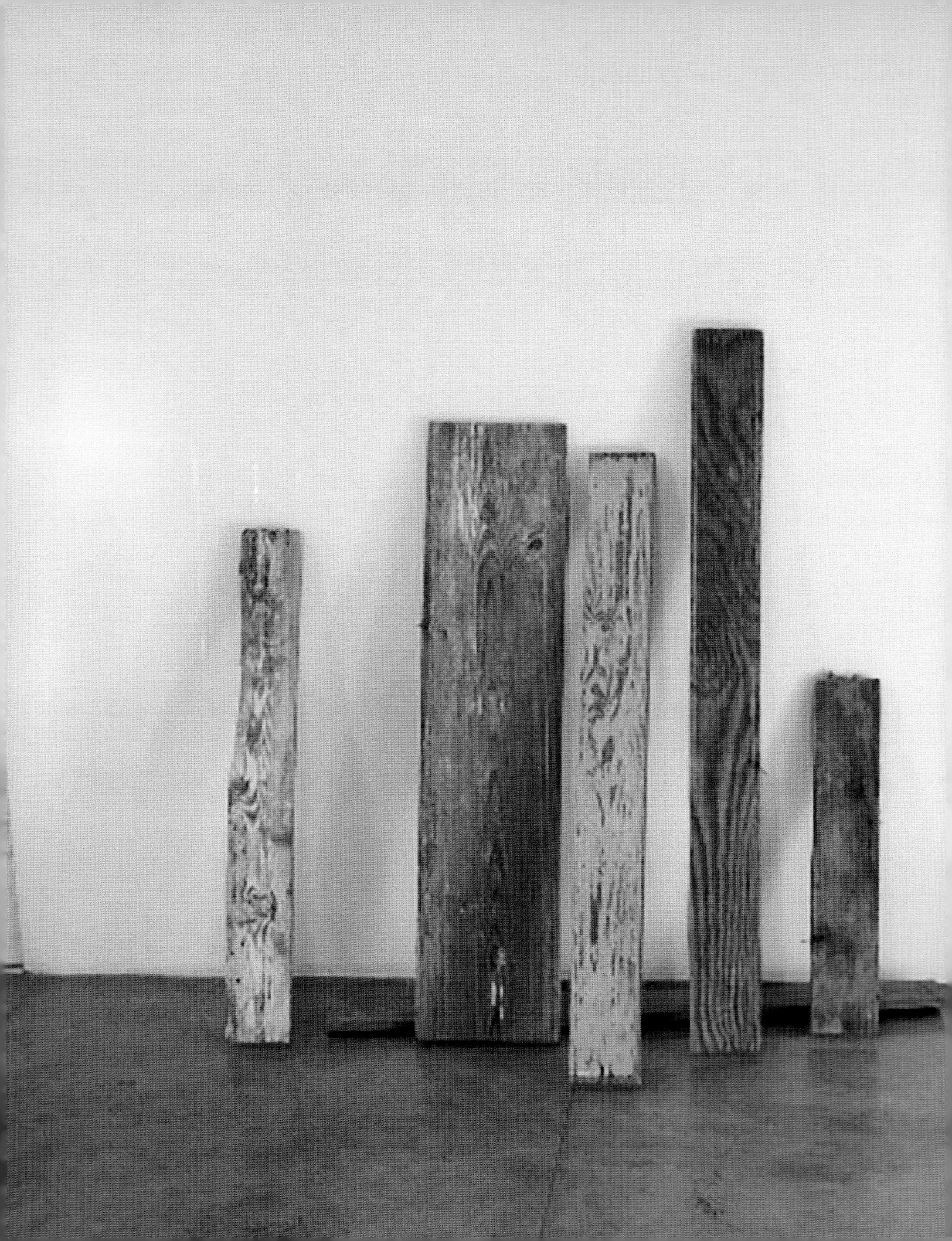

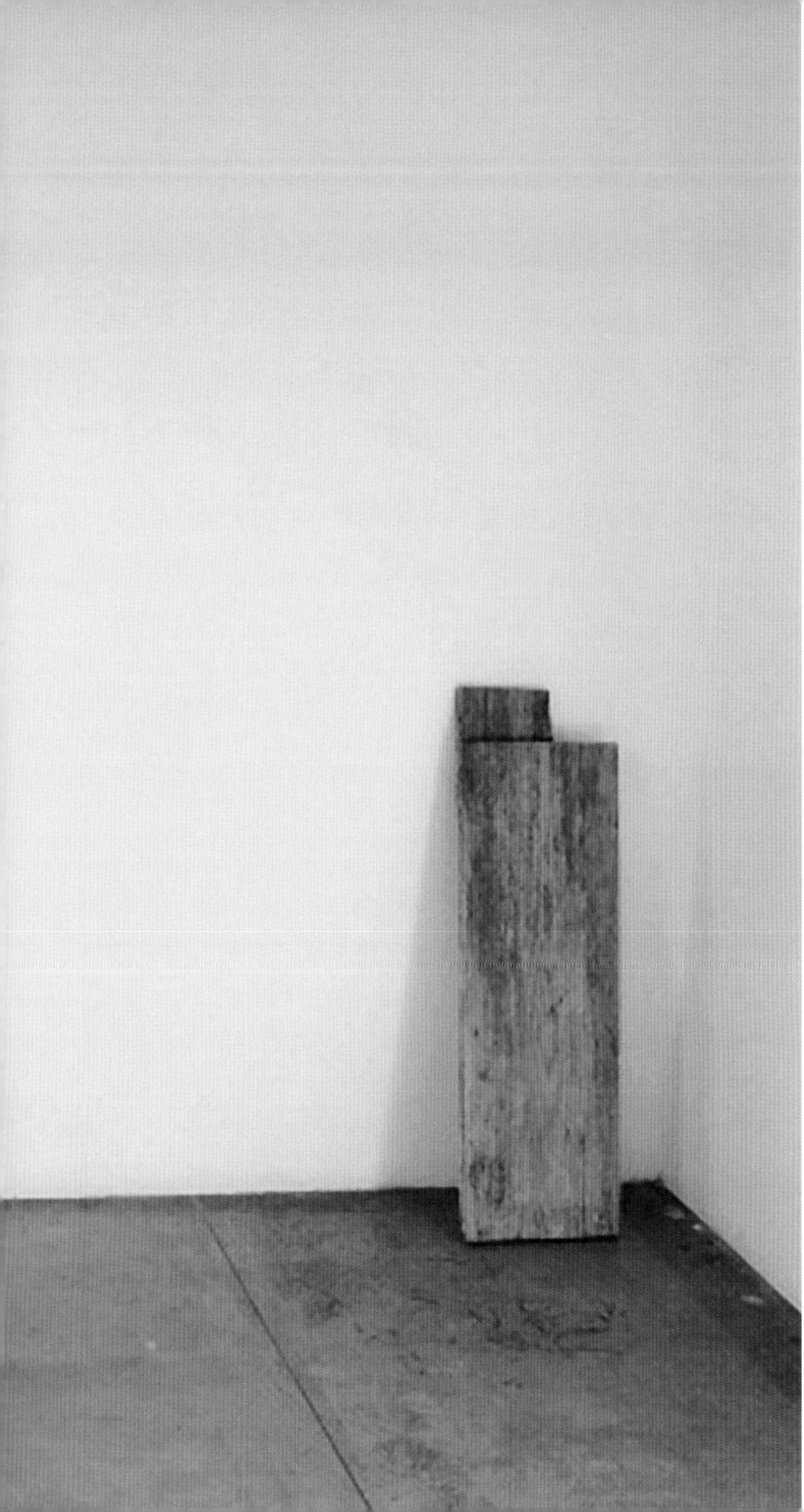

Shadow of a Doubt 2004

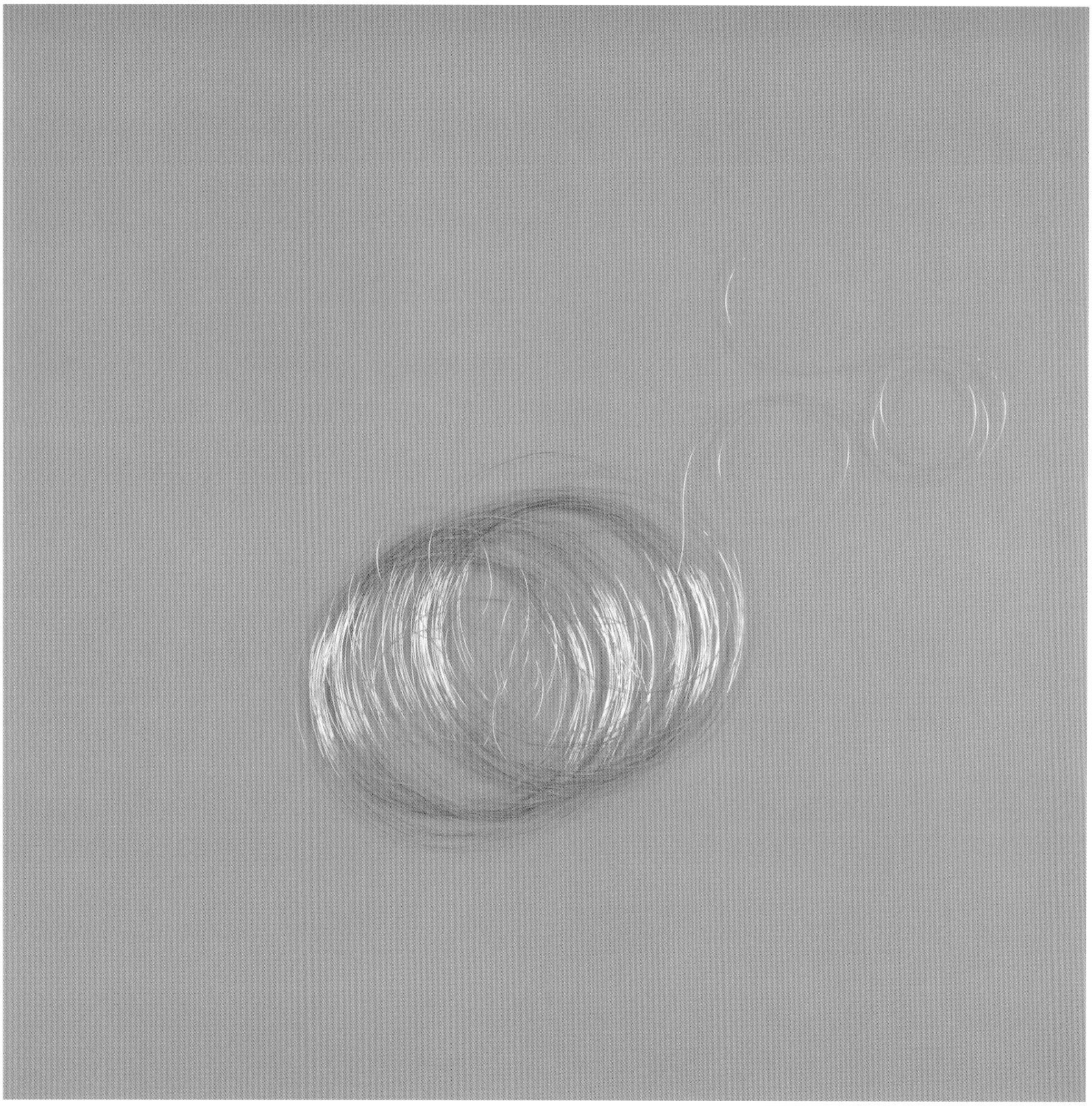

 Measuring Niagara with a Teaspoon 2005

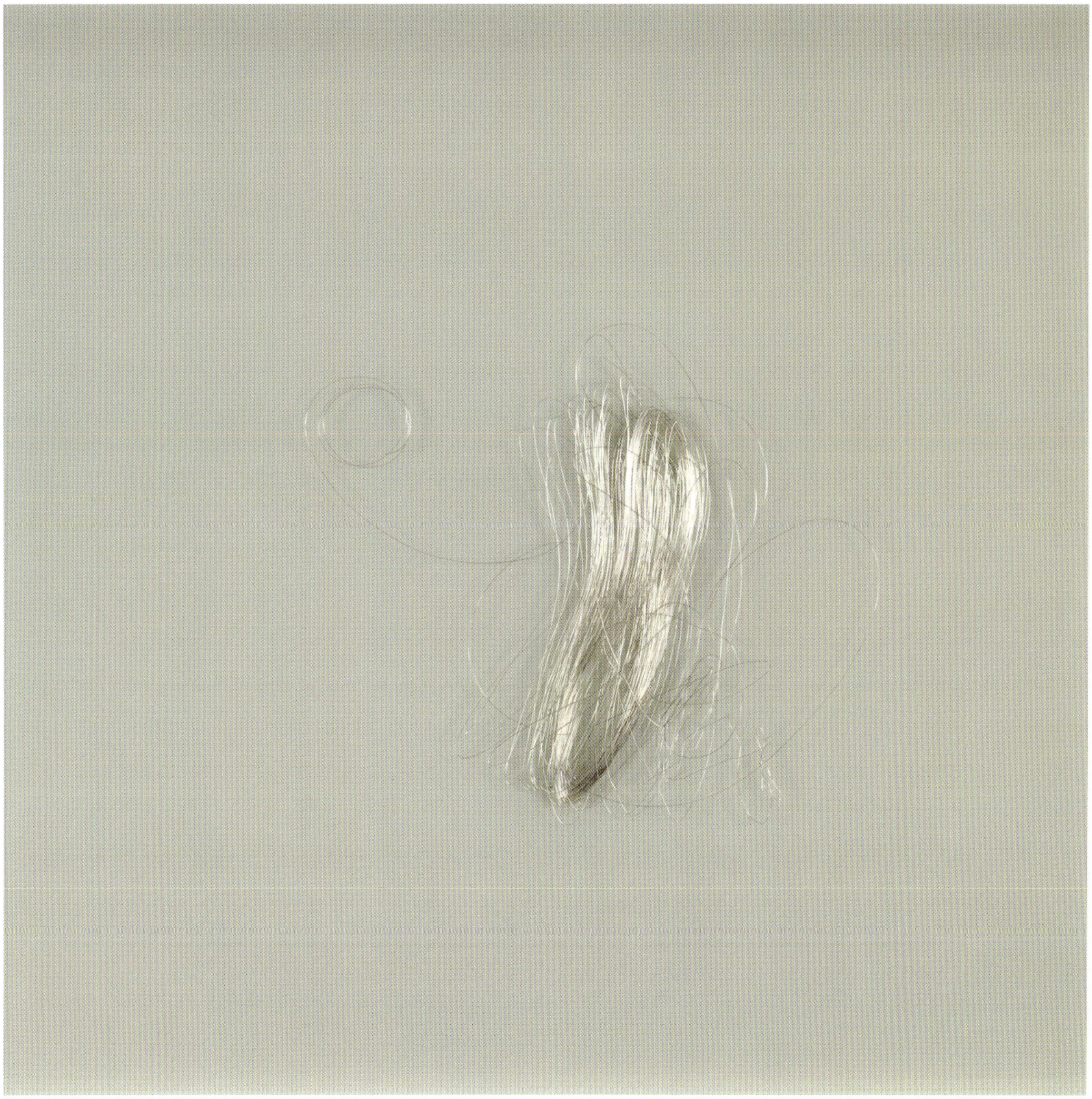

Measuring Liberty with a Dollar 2007

Endless Column III 2006

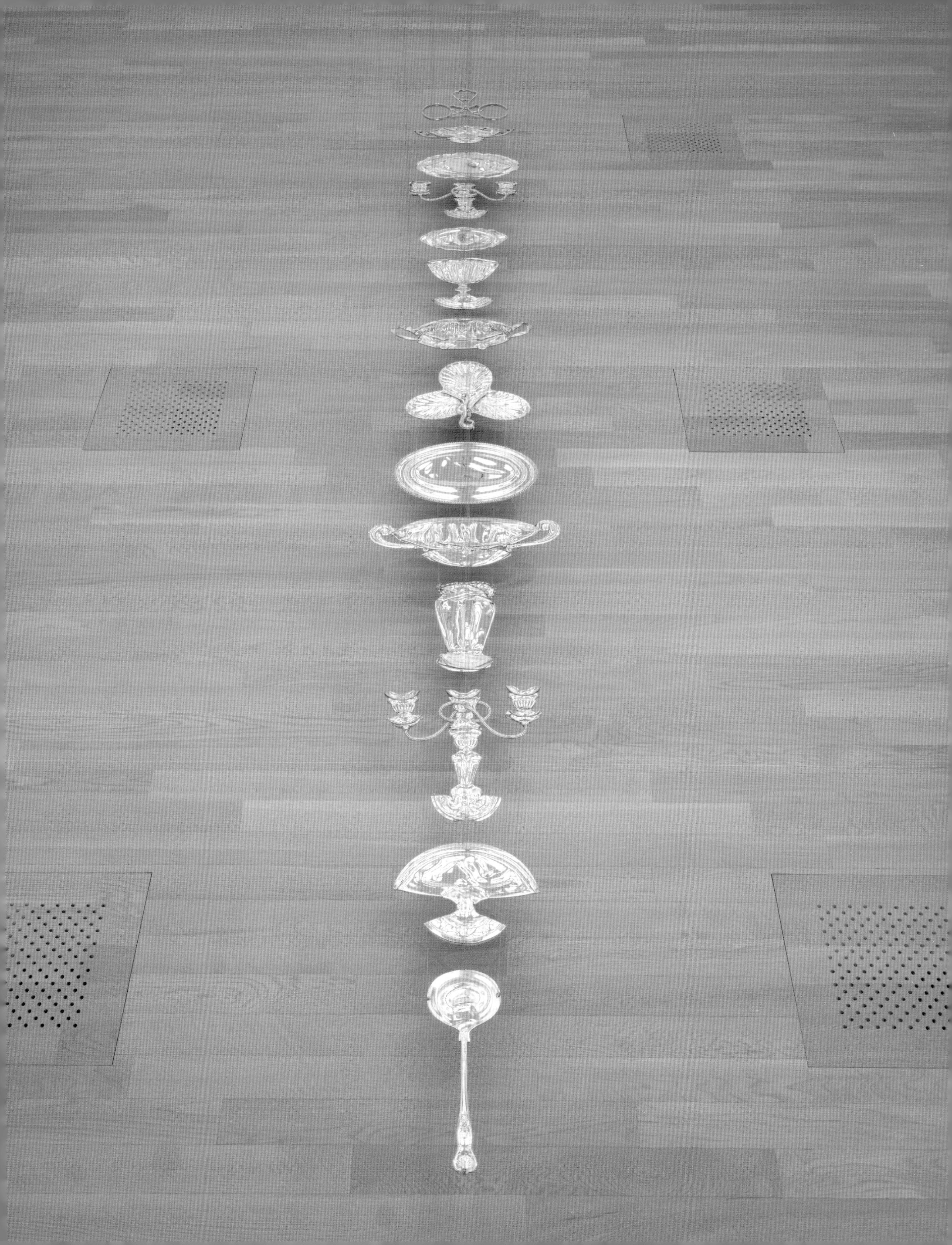

Brontëan Abstract 2006
(deletions from the original manuscripts of Jane Eye)

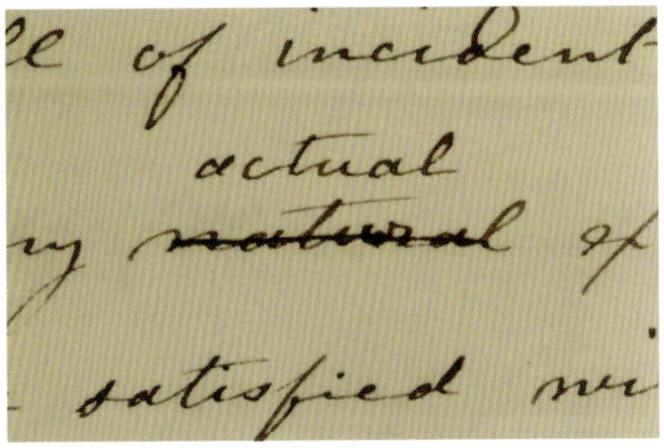
of incident
actual
natural
satisfied

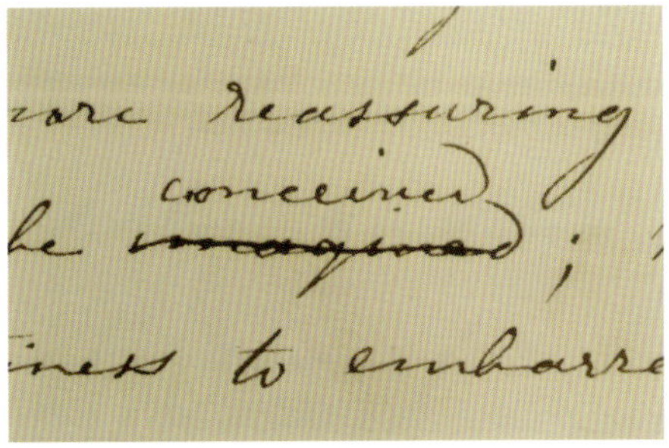
reassuring
conceived
imagined
to embarrass

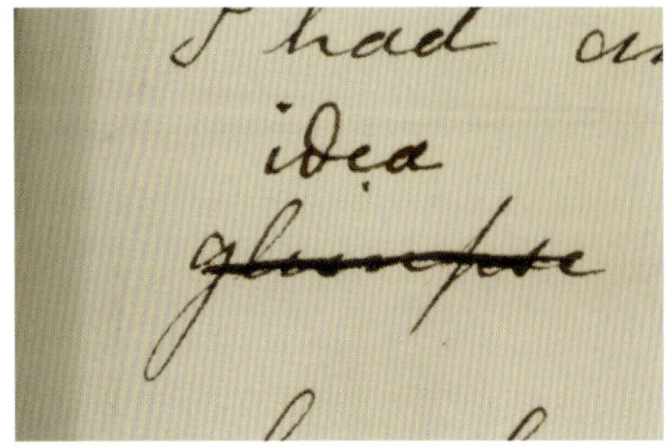
I had
idea
glimpse

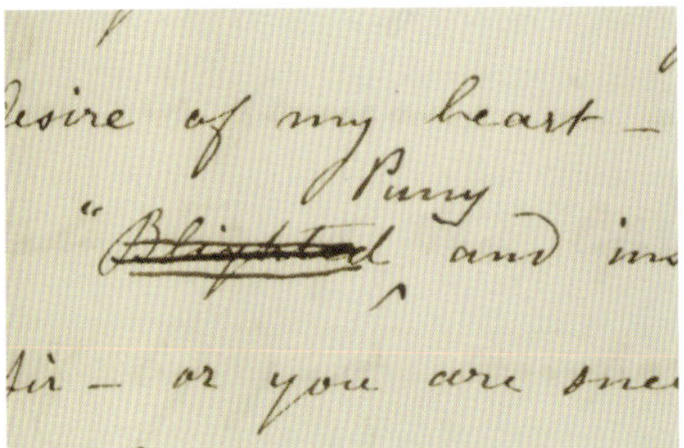
of my heart
Puny
"Blighted, and
or you are

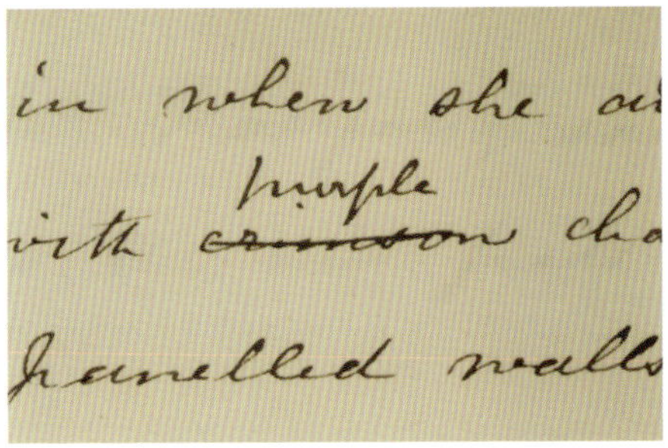
in when she
purple
crimson
panelled walls

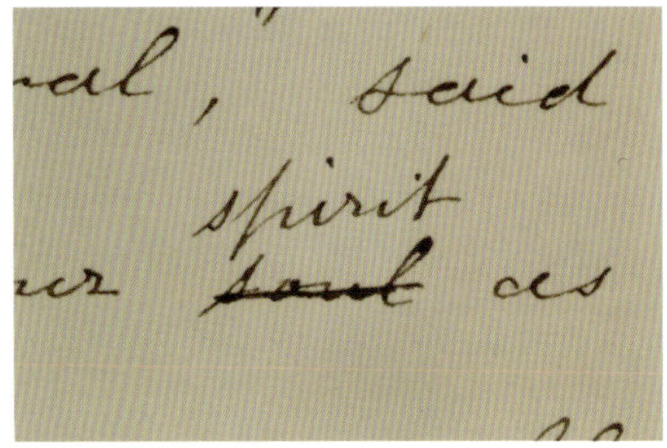
said
spirit
soul
as

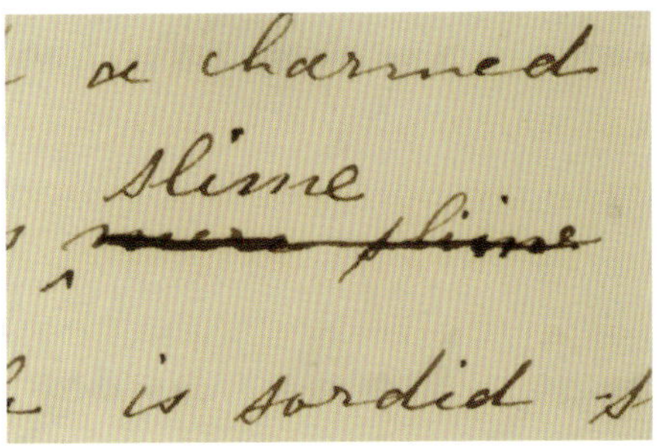
charmed
slime
slime
is sordid

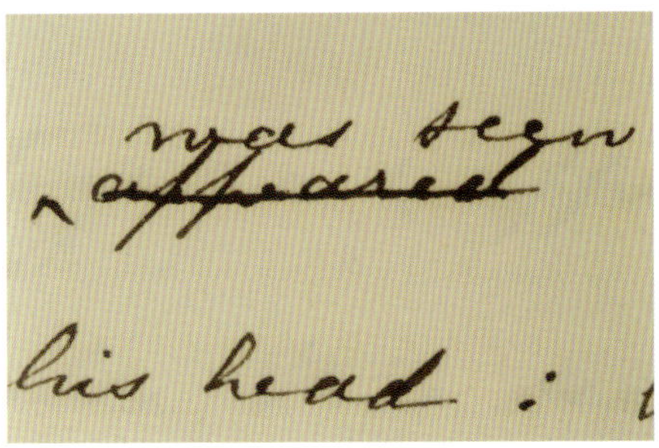
was seen
appeared
his head :

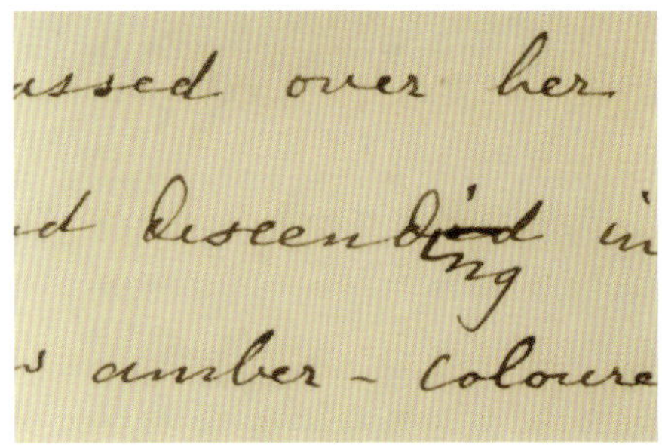
over her
descending
amber-coloured

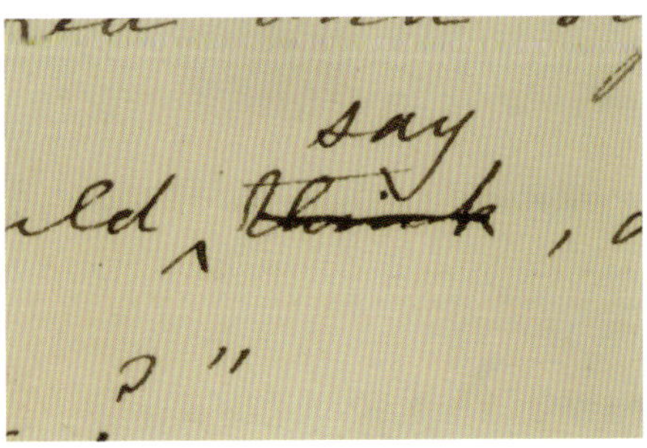
say
think

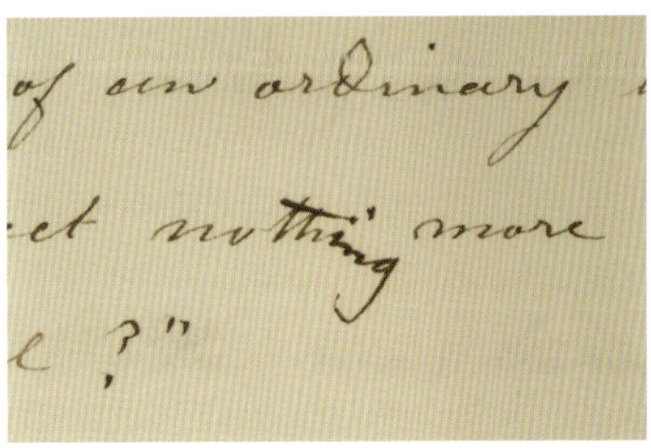
of an ordinary
nothing more

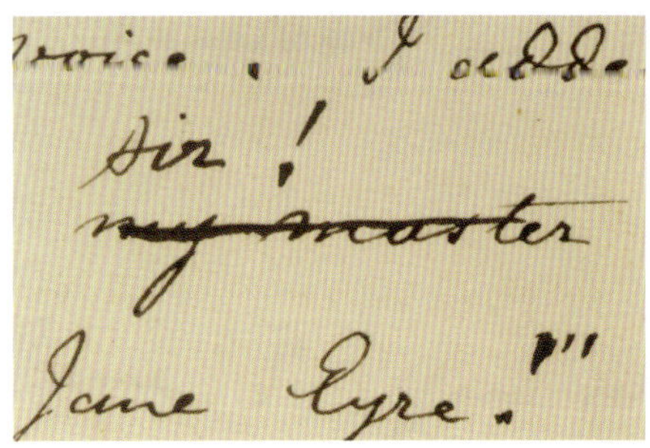
Sir!
my master
Jane Eyre."

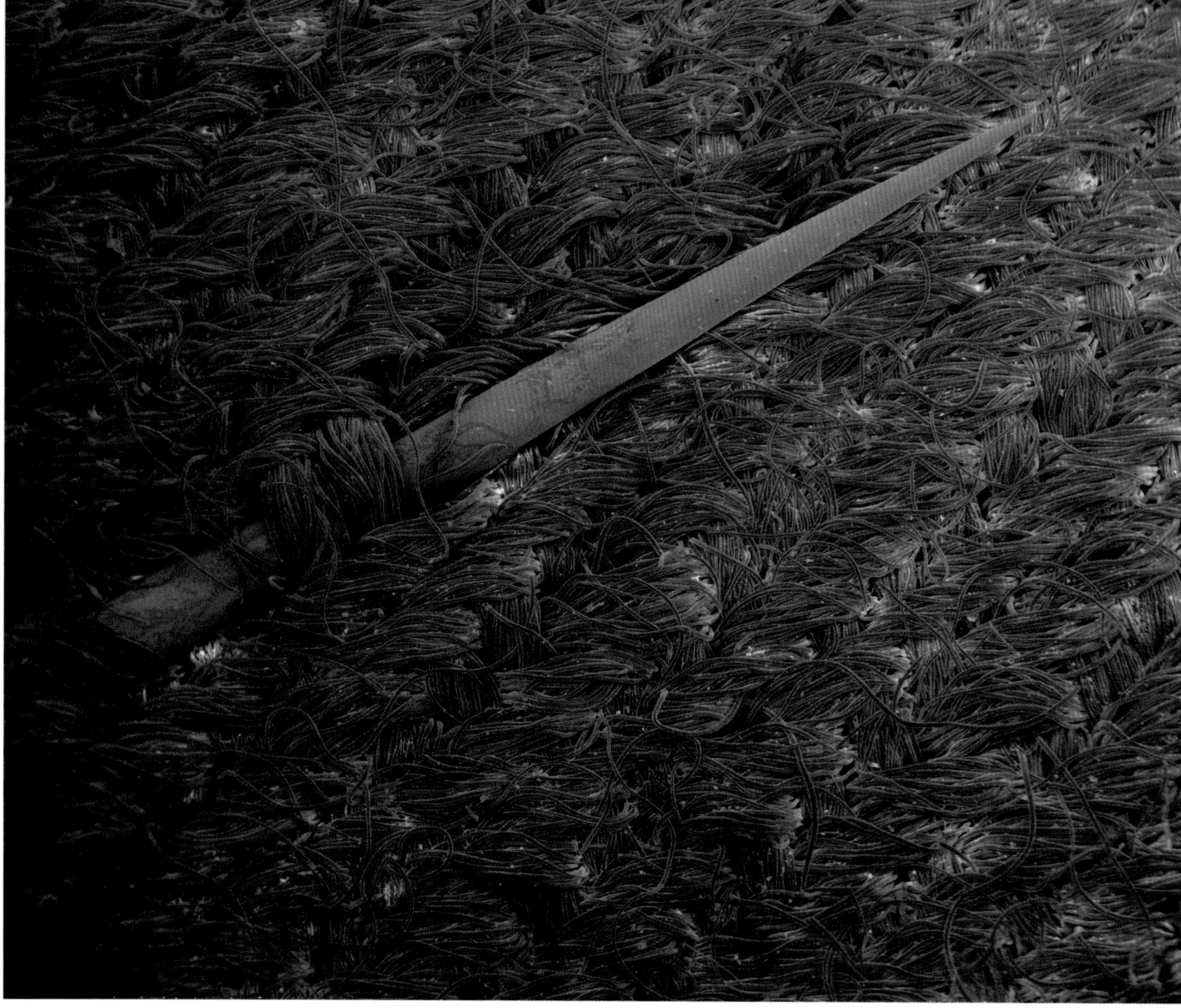

Brontëan Abstract 2006
(Anne Brontë's needle)

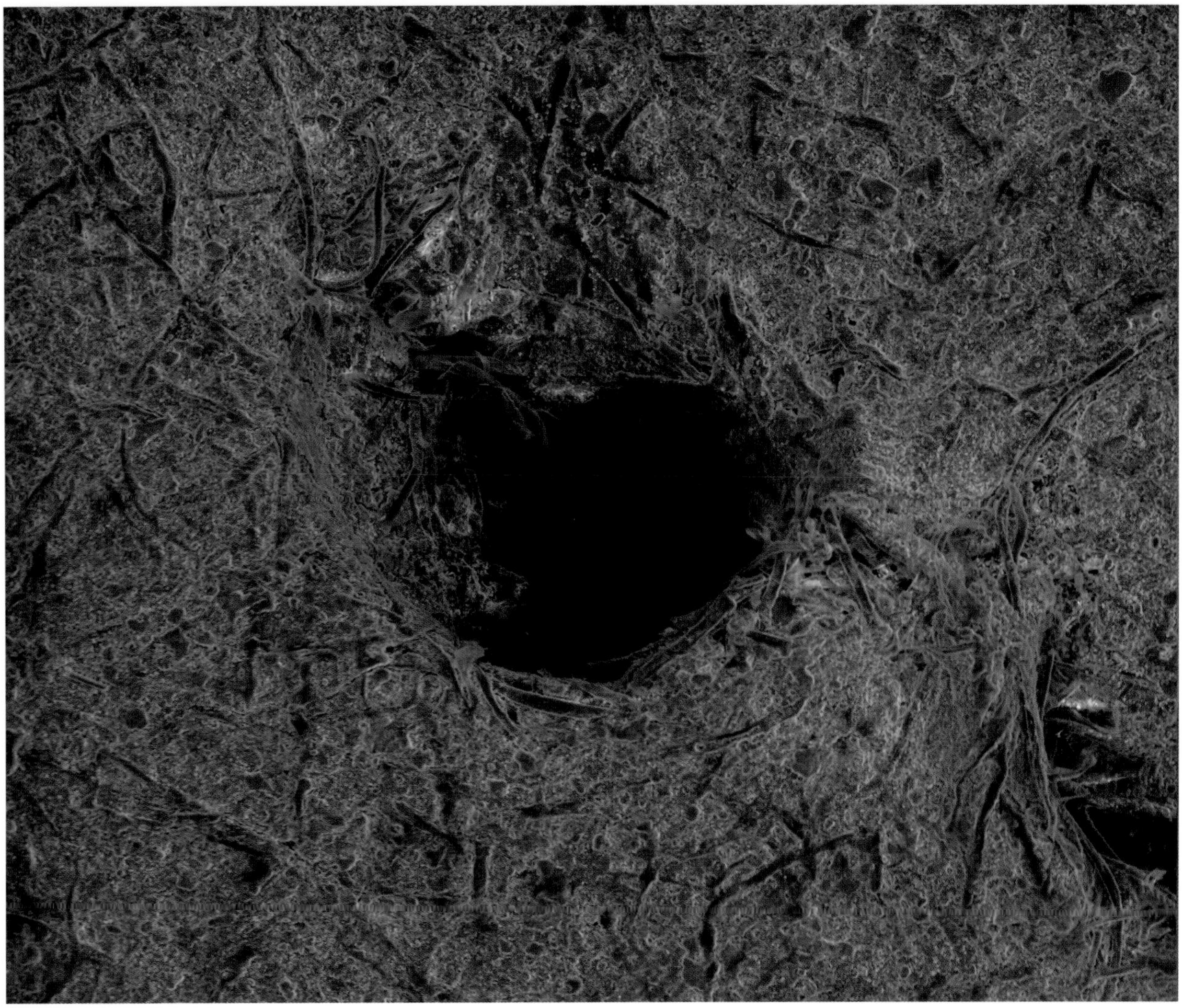

Brontëan Abstract 2006
(pinhole made by Charlotte Brontë)

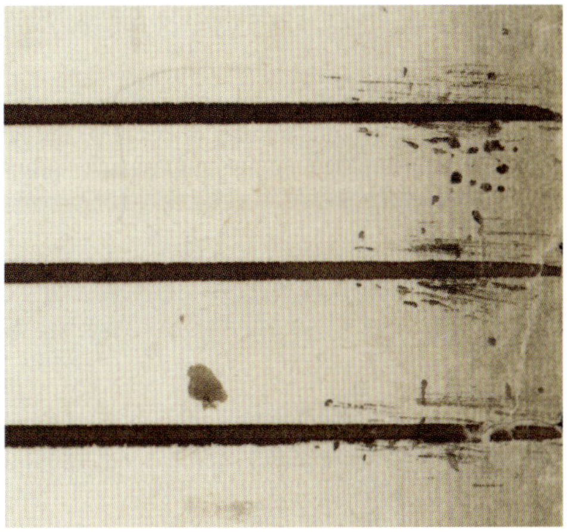

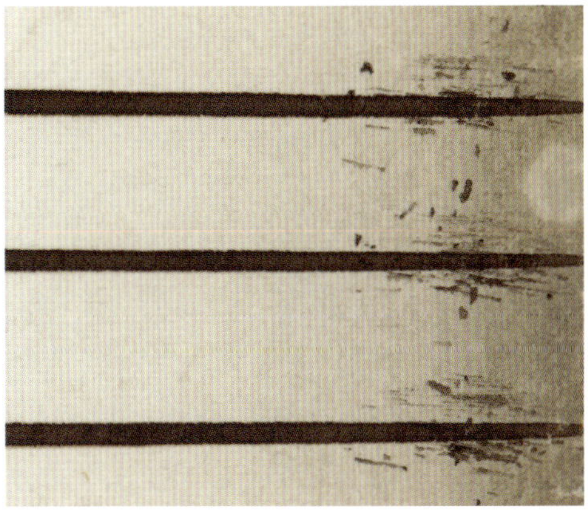

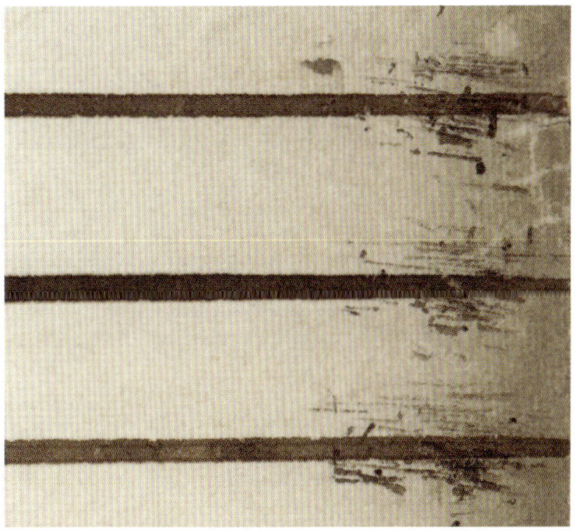

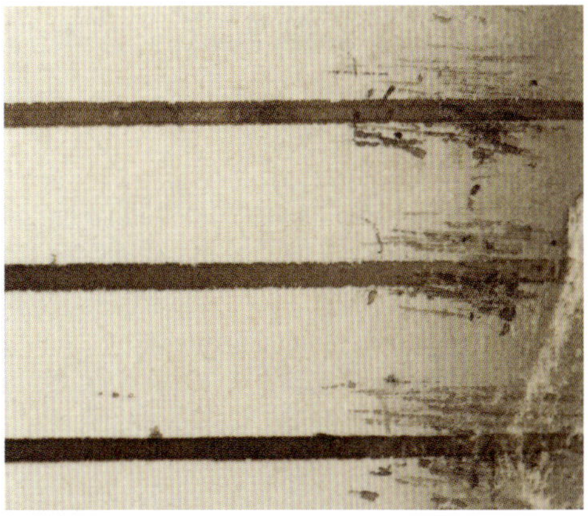

left:
Brontëan Abstract 2006
(Emily Brontë's blotting paper)

right:
Brontëan Abstract 2006
(marks made in the margins by Emily Brontë)

Brontëan Abstract 2006
(Charlotte Brontë's pincushion)

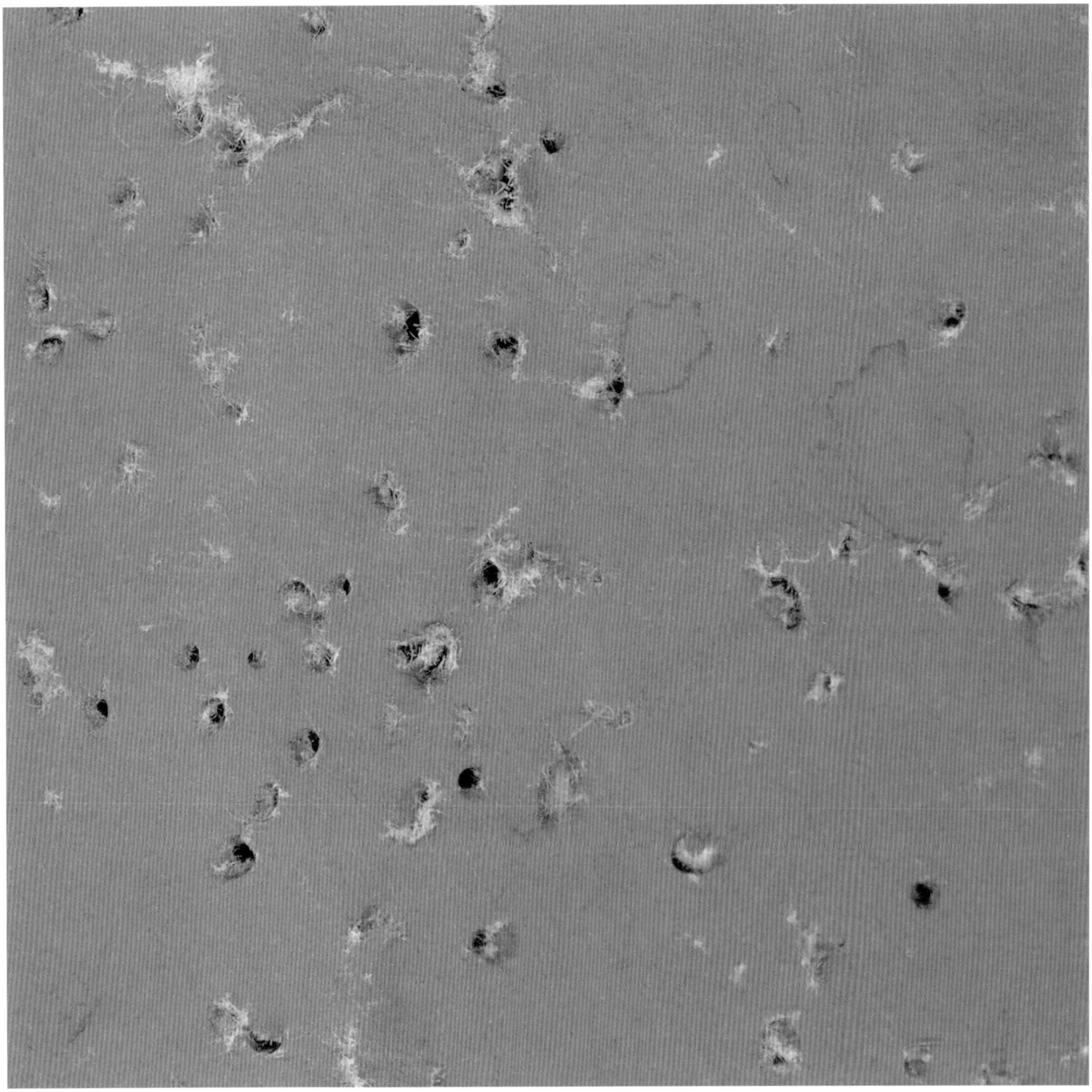

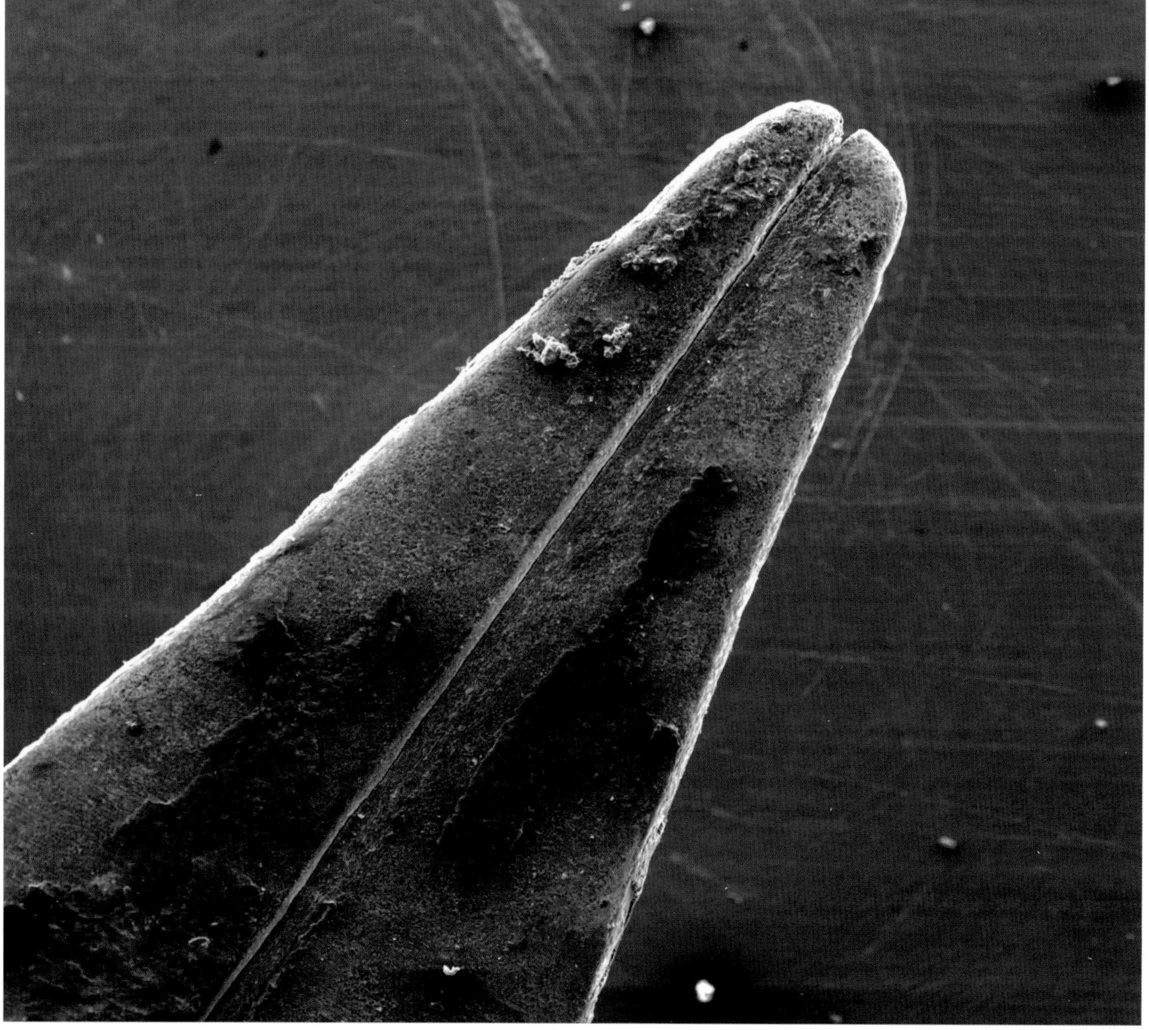

Brontëan Abstract 2006
(Charlotte Brontë's pen nib)

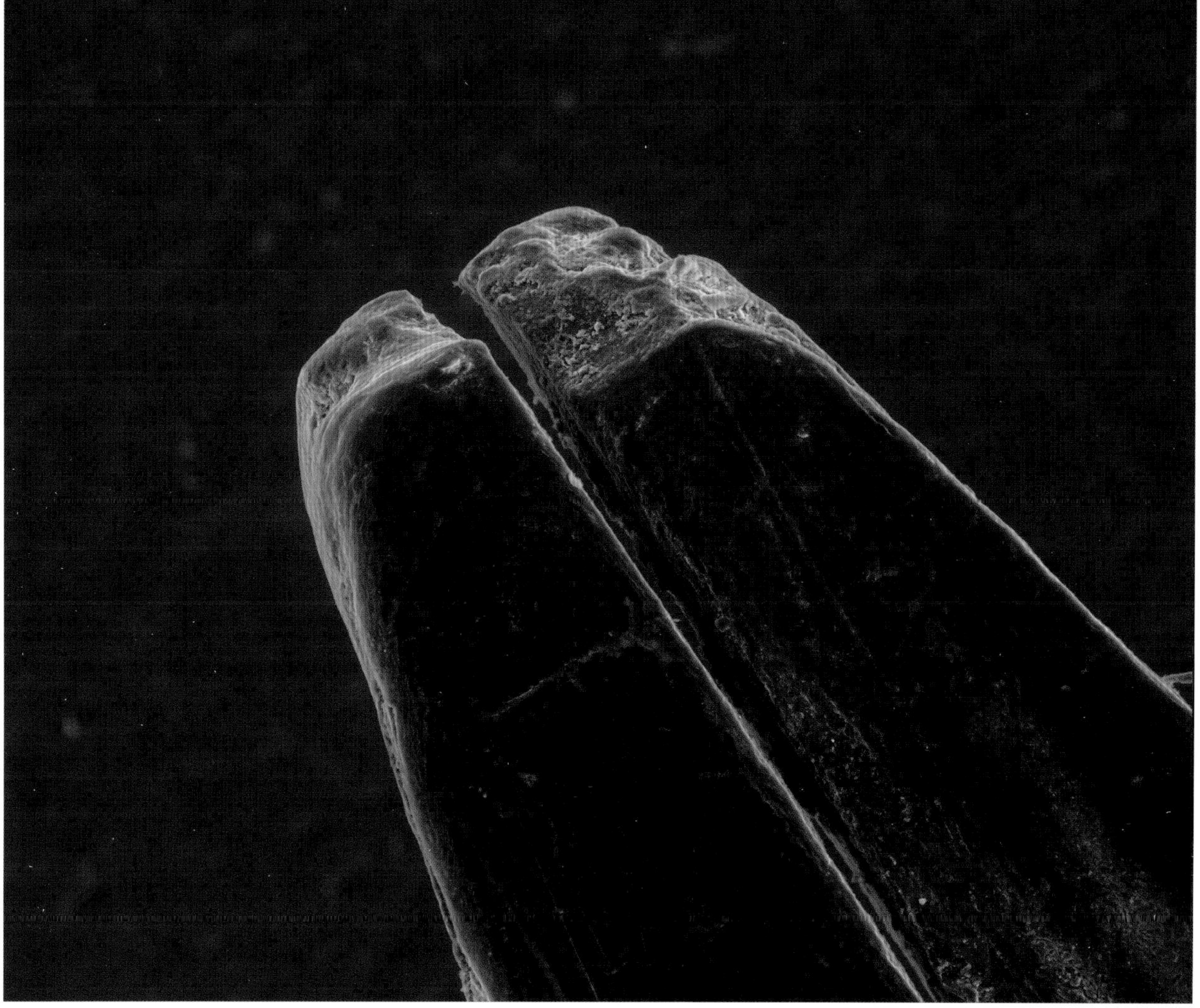

Brontëan Abstract 2006
(Emily Brontë's quill nib)

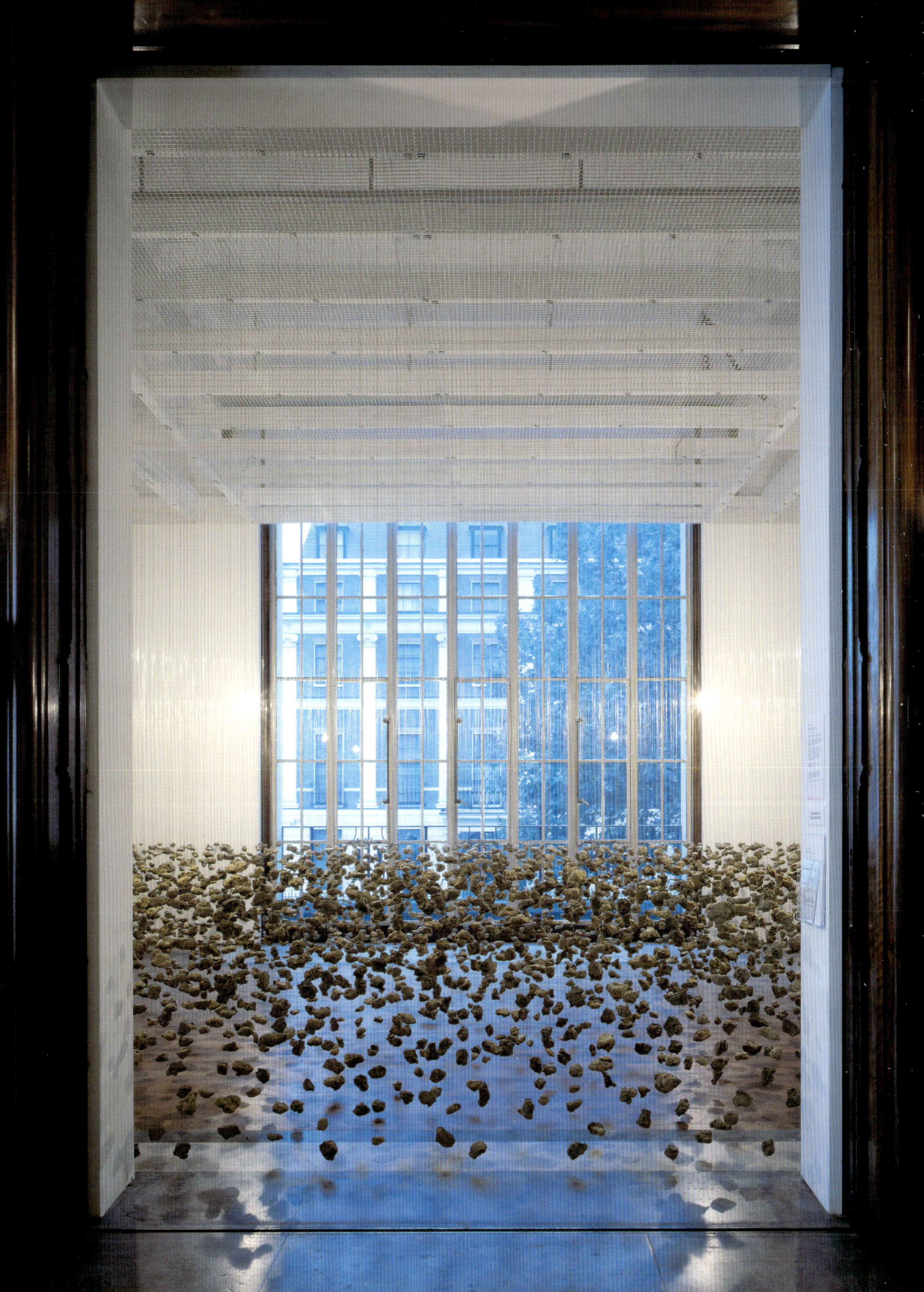

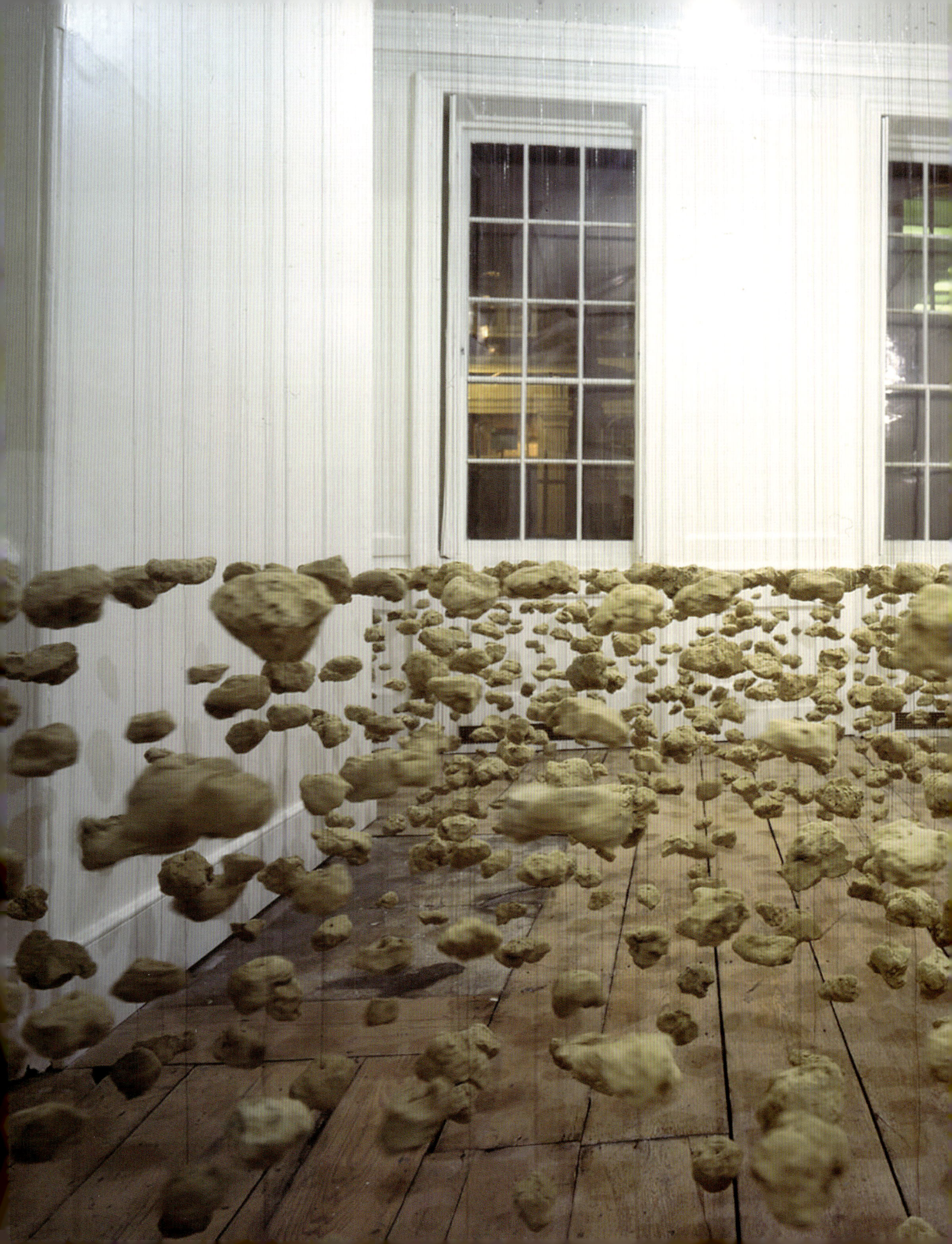

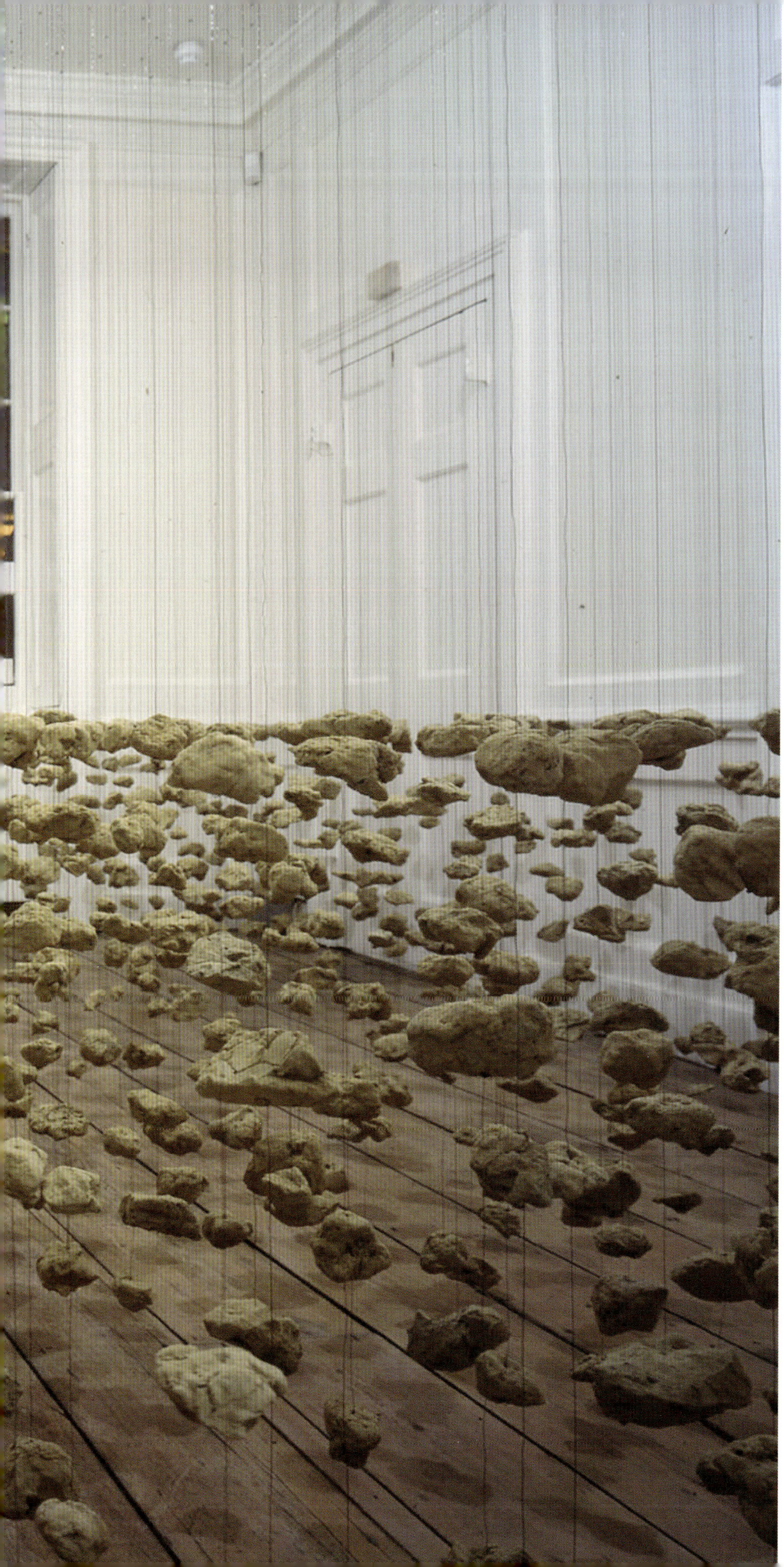

Subconscious of a Monument 2002

Professor Noam Chomsky responding to questions asked by Cornelia Parker at Massachusetts Institute of Technology, 9 March 2007

CP

NC Not just so much of the developed world but the American population, which has also been clamouring for action. In fact, support for, say, the Kyoto protocol, is so overwhelming that a majority of Bush voters thought that he supported it, because it's such an obvious thing to support. But there's a huge gap in the United States between public policy and public opinion… and not just on this issue – on a huge range of issues – so public opinion is pretty much excluded from influence on policy. As a result, even the very strong support for the public does not enter into policy choices, on this or other issues.

As far as the Bush Administration is concerned, their position is the familiar one of corporate executives – which is the sector of the population that they represent, in effect. If you're a CEO of a corporation you don't pay much attention to what's going to happen five years from now. You pay attention to the bottom line in the next quarter… that's going to determine your salary, your prestige, the power of your corporation, and so on. If it turns out that the world is going to collapse five years from now, that's somebody else's business.

Governments reflect the interests of their populations, to some extent at least. And people, of course, would like a world for their grandchildren to live in – so therefore they have different points of view. But the very same individual as a State manager and as a human being may make very different choices. You can see this when people drop out of office and they come at the world from a different point of view. There are many such conflicts. I mean, even though the Government is extremely closely linked to major corporations, in particular energy corporations (so the Bush Administration practically comes out of the energy sector) – even though there's a very tight linkage, there are conflicts – striking conflicts – when the same individual, say Dick Cheney, is representing corporate interests or State interests – and sometimes it's almost comical. Just to give a minor example… or, pick a major example, which illustrates it… take an impending war with Iran. Corporations aren't in favour of it; the population's overwhelmingly opposed; the energy corporations would be pleased to enter into Iran and exploit its oil resources – but the US Government won't allow them because it has a State interest. The State interest goes back to a standard Mafia-style of international affairs… the Godfather does not accept disobedience; it has to be punished.

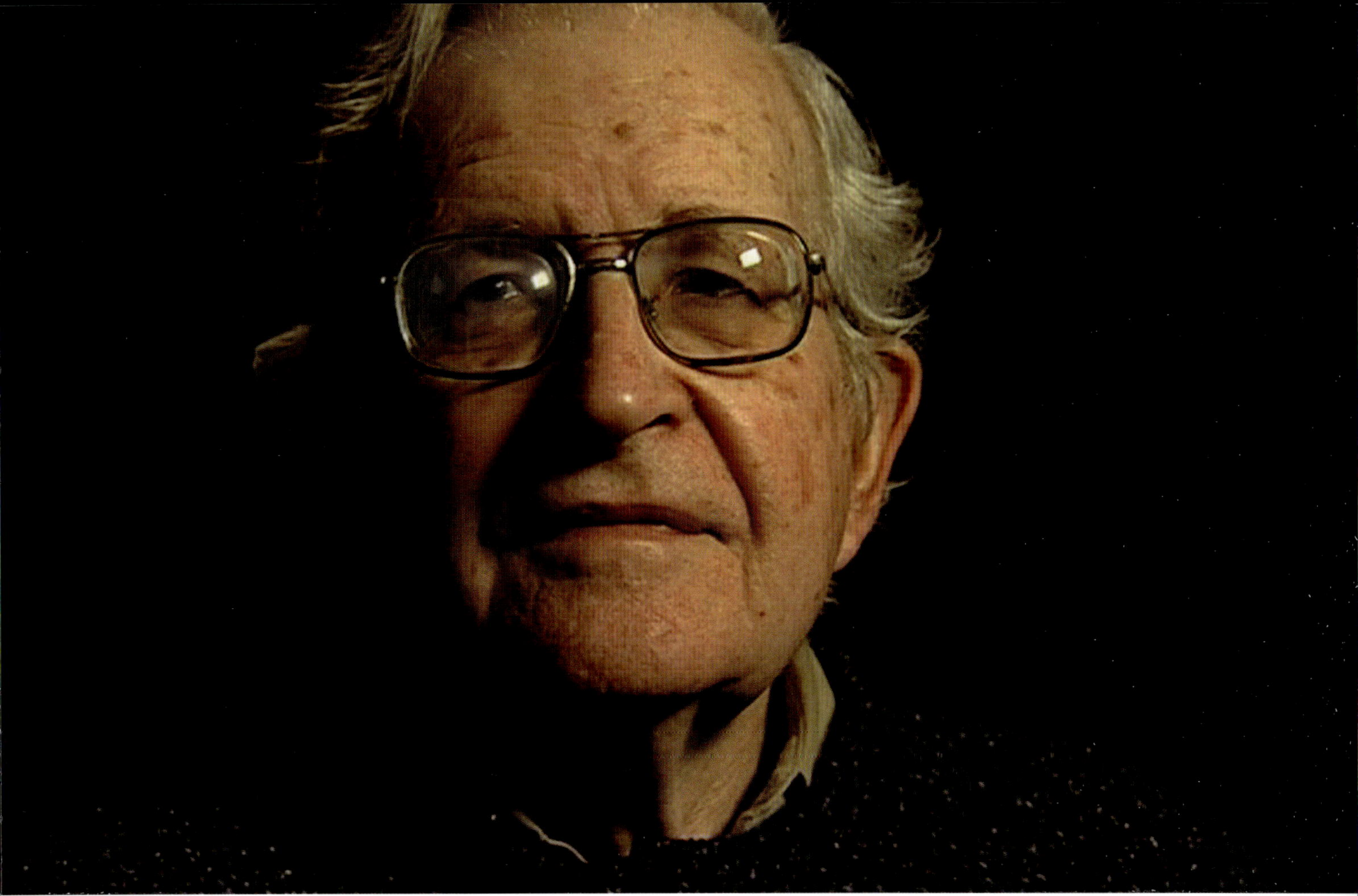

And, in 1979, Iran was disobedient. They overthrew a US-imposed tyrant, who was a centrepiece of US power in the region and, what's more, they even put some American diplomats in prison... so then all of US-Iranian history, which was horrible, is eliminated – and we've got to punish the Iranians for that. The US immediately started supporting Saddam Hussein's war against Iran, went on with harsh sanctions... and the energy corporations can't break through that, even though the Administration comes straight from that sector. In fact, there are even more dramatic cases... take, say, Cuba. The US has been punishing Cuba (or Cubans, not Cuba – the people of Cuba) for 45 years because of what internal documents call "successful defiance" – their successful defiance of US policies going back to the Monroe Doctrine. The Godfather does not accept that. Successful defiance is intolerable. People have to be punished to ensure that they overthrow the Government that is defying the master. The population of the United States – large majorities – want to establish diplomatic relations with Cuba... end the embargo, end the terror, and so on and so forth – it's been true for decades.

A lot of the business world wants to do the same thing – they see market opportunities – and, particularly interesting, is the oil companies...

Texas oil companies, (George Bush's background) want to exploit offshore Cuban oil. US Government, which comes right out of that sector, won't allow them to do it. Sometimes it reaches comic proportions. About a year ago, there was a meeting in Mexico between Cuban energy officials and Texas oil company executives (including some of the bigger ones, like Exxon Mobil). Washington discovered that it was being held in a Sheraton Hotel, which is owned in the United States, and they ordered the hotel to throw them out. Now, here you have George Bush and his friends coming out of the Texas oil industry, you have their friends – the Texas oil industry – trying to reduce US dependency on foreign oil by exploiting closer oil... but, in his capacity (whoever makes the decisions)... in their capacity as State executives, the US is perfectly willing to shoot themselves in the foot to prevent use of oil nearby, to harm their constituency, in order to ensure that successful defiance will not be tolerated. Now, any Mafia Don will understand this. And those kinds of conflicts exist.

In the case of the global warming, for the real constituency of the Bush Administration, the energy corporations, multi-nationals and so on... they don't care that much what happens. In their capacity in those institutions it doesn't matter if their grandchildren don't have a world to live in. Of course, when they go home, it does matter. But people act differently in institutional frameworks.

CP

NC Yes, he's correct – but it's far more general. Take, say, lead... it was known that lead was poisonous by the early 1920s. It took 50 years in the United States before you could get some legislation to protect children from dying from lead poisoning. It was done... but the facts were known... companies were keeping a lot of it secret, but most of it was known. 50 years. Take tobacco it has never been technically criminalized. But there are now measures, which make it difficult for children to smoke. It's been known for decades that tobacco is far more lethal than hard drugs – incomparably more lethal – but the major corporations and the media, which go along with them, have held it back. Now take, say, Europe – I read recently, in an article, a book by Hugh O'Shaughnessy a British journalist, that the European Union subsidy for tobacco industries is greater than the amount of money that the European Union provides for alternative crops for people growing coca. That's supposed to be one of the ways to stop drug production – provide them with alternative crops. They get less money for that than the British tobacco companies, and the others, get for poisoning people at a level far beyond that of hard drugs. Well, you know, those are the short-term calculations of people whose institutional role is to maximize profit, market share and power... . whatever they may think – you know, move outside, they may be the nicest people in the world...

I remember once, when the Butcher of Lyon was captured – Klaus Barbie – finally captured... He had worked for the Nazis and then the Americans picked him up. He was doing exactly the same work for the Americans and they finally spirited him off to Latin America – he was becoming

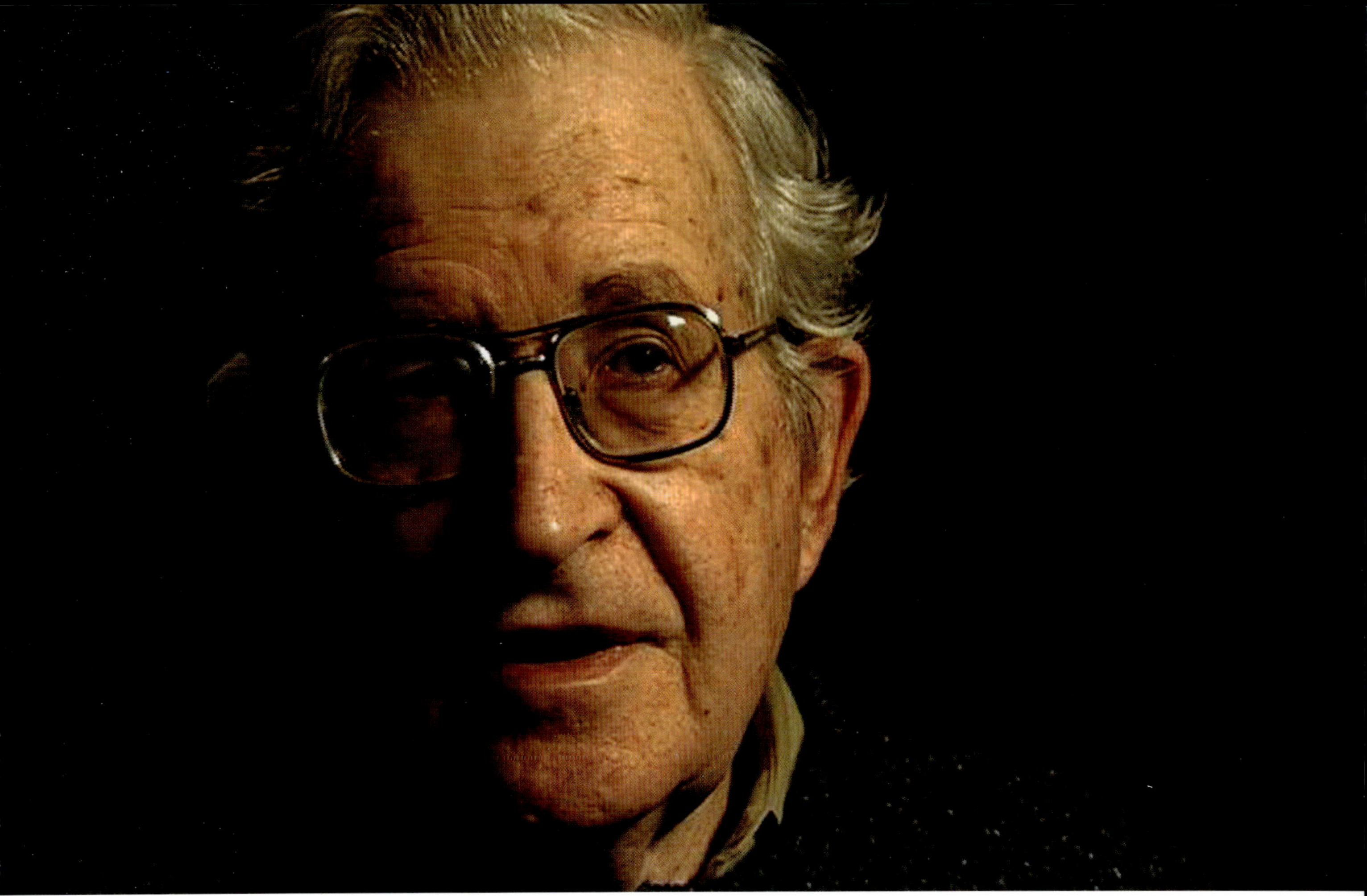

embarrassing… but he was finally picked up and he was taken to France – he was going to be tried. I happened to be listening to the, I think it was probably the National Public Radio. They had an interview with his daughter. She said she didn't believe any of the charges against him because he was the nicest father in the world and he was very loving, took care of everybody… a sweet guy, and so on… which I think is probably perfectly true. You can be one thing at home and you can be something else in an institutional role. You can be destroying the world in your institutional role – consciously – and loving your children at home.

Case after case of poison and destruction and so on has this property. The same is true of what you began with – Apocalypse Soon – which was not my phrase; it was Robert McNamara's… so when a sober or serious analyst warns of apocalypse soon, it is correct. Unlike climate change… we may be past the point when we can solve it… maybe mitigate it, but something bad's going to happen… In the case of nuclear war, which is far more dangerous – I mean, that terminates the species – we know what to do, how to solve it… I mean, it's not a mystery, the solution is understood but it's just not interesting, so we'll take the chance, the serious chance, of apocalypse soon or "Armageddon of our own making" as Senator Sam Nunn put it, because it's more important to be able to shake our fist at people.

CP

NC If you take an Economics course, they teach you that a market, a consumer market, is based on informed consumers making rational choices. Right? Then you have rational choice theory and you go on from there. Well, have you ever turned on a television set? Yes, I suppose so. You've seen an advertisement… let's say, for an automobile or a lifestyle drug or toothpaste. I mean, is the advertisement giving you information about the product? No. I mean, if they were giving information about the… if they're trying to have informed consumers they'd say here's specification for model so-and-so next year. Instead, it's doing exactly what Adam Smith said is the job of business: to delude and oppress the public. He was correct. The goal of business is to delude and oppress the public. And they delude the public by not telling you what this automobile is but having a beautiful actress, say, sitting on top of it… or climbing up some impossible mountain, or something like that. Business is spending hundreds of millions of dollars a year to undermine the threat of markets with informed consumers making rational choices. They want uninformed consumers to make irrational choices. And, on top of that, they want to fabricate consumers – create 'wants' – as the business literature points out.

So, at either end, we don't really have market systems – and it goes on… I mean, take what's called 'trade'. It's largely an economist's myth. I mean, in the old Soviet Union, if something was produced – if parts were produced – in Leningrad then send to Bulgaria for assembly and then the automobile was sold in Poland, it crossed borders but we didn't call it trade – it was all within a command economy. Well, when General Motors produces parts in Indiana, sends them to Mexico for assembly and sells them in California, we call it trade in both directions – but it's internal to a command economy. It's not trade in any meaningful sense – and it's certainly not free trade. In fact, free trade is the last thing that States want. If you take a phrase like North American Free Trade Agreement, the only accurate words in it are 'North American'. It wasn't an agreement either, if people count as part of their countries, because most people were against it. You just have to decode an awful lot of mythology before you can even talk about these questions.

CP

NC Oh, I think so. In fact, it's… the fact that consumption is sort of the goal of life was manufactured – consciously. If you go back to the business literature in the 1920s, and ever since in an increasing scale, it was recognized that we must (I'm almost quoting) focus people on the superficial things of life – like fashionable consumption. If we don't do that, they're going to get involved in the political system… and we don't want that. What was happening in, roughly, the 1920s, is that, in the most free countries of the world – Britain and the United States – enough freedom had been won so that it was becoming impossible for the State to control people by force, in the old way. You were getting parliamentary Labour parties, women were getting the right to vote, and the vulgar masses were getting involved in running their own affairs – which cannot be

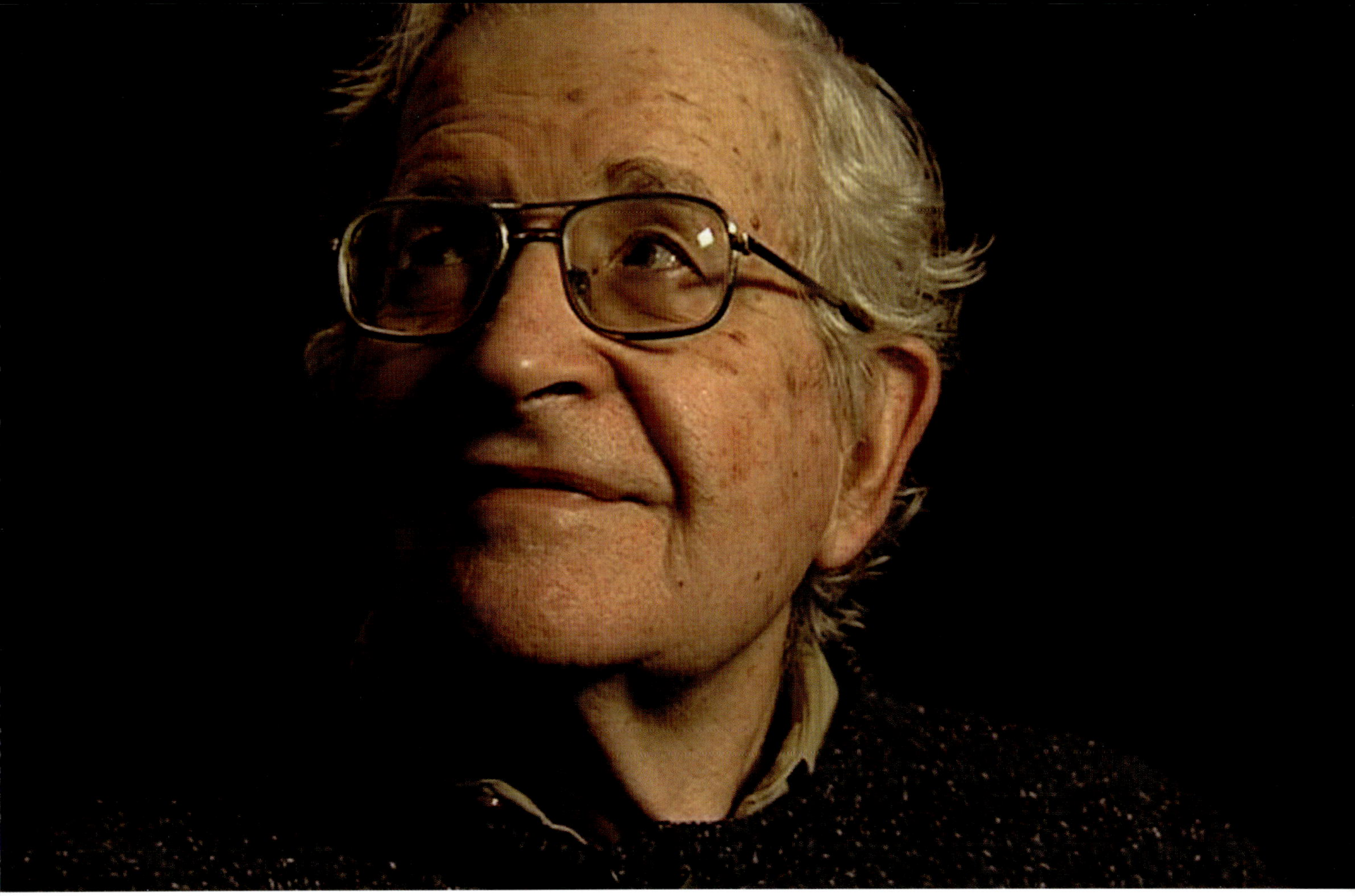

tolerated. You couldn't control them by force. That's when conceptions like manufacturing consent, or fabricating consumers, and engineering of consent, were developed. That's when the public relations industry developed... in the freest countries – in the United States and Britain. And its main goal was to create consumerism, first of all, because it's profitable, but also, because it's anti-democratic. Invariably the main goal of business, and other elites, is to undermine democracy – which is regarded as very threatening.

Actually, I should say that elections in the United States are now run the same way that commodities are sold – and by the same institutions, so it's not accidental. So you undermine markets by creating uninformed consumers making irrational choices – and the same public relations institutions, when they run elections (look at the ads), try to do the same thing: keep away from issues; present imagery, delusion; and so on. You don't want people to pay attention to issues because, on issues, the public disagrees enormously with the two factions of the business party. So keep issues out of it. People don't know the stands of the candidate on issues. You focus on whether he's a nice guy, you'd like to meet him at a bar, does Hilary Clinton have too much of a sex problem or... I don't know, whatever it may be – but those are the things you focus on, just take a look at the newspapers or television… and it's very much like undermining markets. But this came in the free societies as a result of the victory of struggles to attain democracy, which is frightening. It has to be beaten back. Consumerism is, to a large extent, created by conscious effort… but that means it's fragile – and it is. And, there are large sectors of society that just don't want it. They want to live a decent lifestyle, not have every imaginable gadget you can have in your home.

Can that develop? Yep, sure – these are cultural changes that can certainly develop. It's never easy to do these things… but, of course, there are no major institutions backing it. It has to be done through popular action. And, at a higher level, at a State level, it has to be done by co-operation with the oil producers and the oil consumers. Actually, I'm sure you know, when Hugo Chávez appeared at the United Nations there was tremendous ridicule of his outrageous speech. He actually gave a very sensible speech at the Security Council, at the General Assembly I guess, which I don't think was ever reported. His speech started by saying exactly this point… he said we are facing an environmental crisis – the oil producers, like my country, and the oil consumers, like many of the others gathered here, have to co-operate to deal with this crisis which will require carrying out significant socio-economic changes… changing the nature of the world order – the way we live and so on – so that we can reduce and maybe end the use of petroleum for production of energy, and use if for more healthy things… and find other ways to live. And he went on with a number of constructive suggestions. Well that, as far as I can recall, didn't even get reported. It's much more interesting to report him calling Bush a devil…

CP

NC Nobody can predict the future of technology, so it makes good sense to explore technological solutions to things like environmental problems but, of course, you can't have faith in them. And you can be pretty confident that any technological solution that comes along will have negative side effects as well, which will have to be balanced.

Nothing comes free. If history's any guide – history of science, too – there is not going to be a magic solution.

It was thought at one point that nuclear power would be a magic solution. It was quickly discovered that there are very harmful negative effects. And it's very likely that that'll be true of any kind of technology that's developed. The cosmos is a complex system, any way you manipulate it, something else is going to happen that you hadn't thought about. So, yes, every such effort should be pursued, if they make any sense, but with recognition that, at the core of the problem is serious socio-economic and cultural changes. We just have to live in other ways, not like the ones that we have been driven to live in. There's nothing natural, nothing in human nature, that forces people to work 20 hours a day to accumulate as many commodities as they can stuff into their house. I mean, that's an imposed

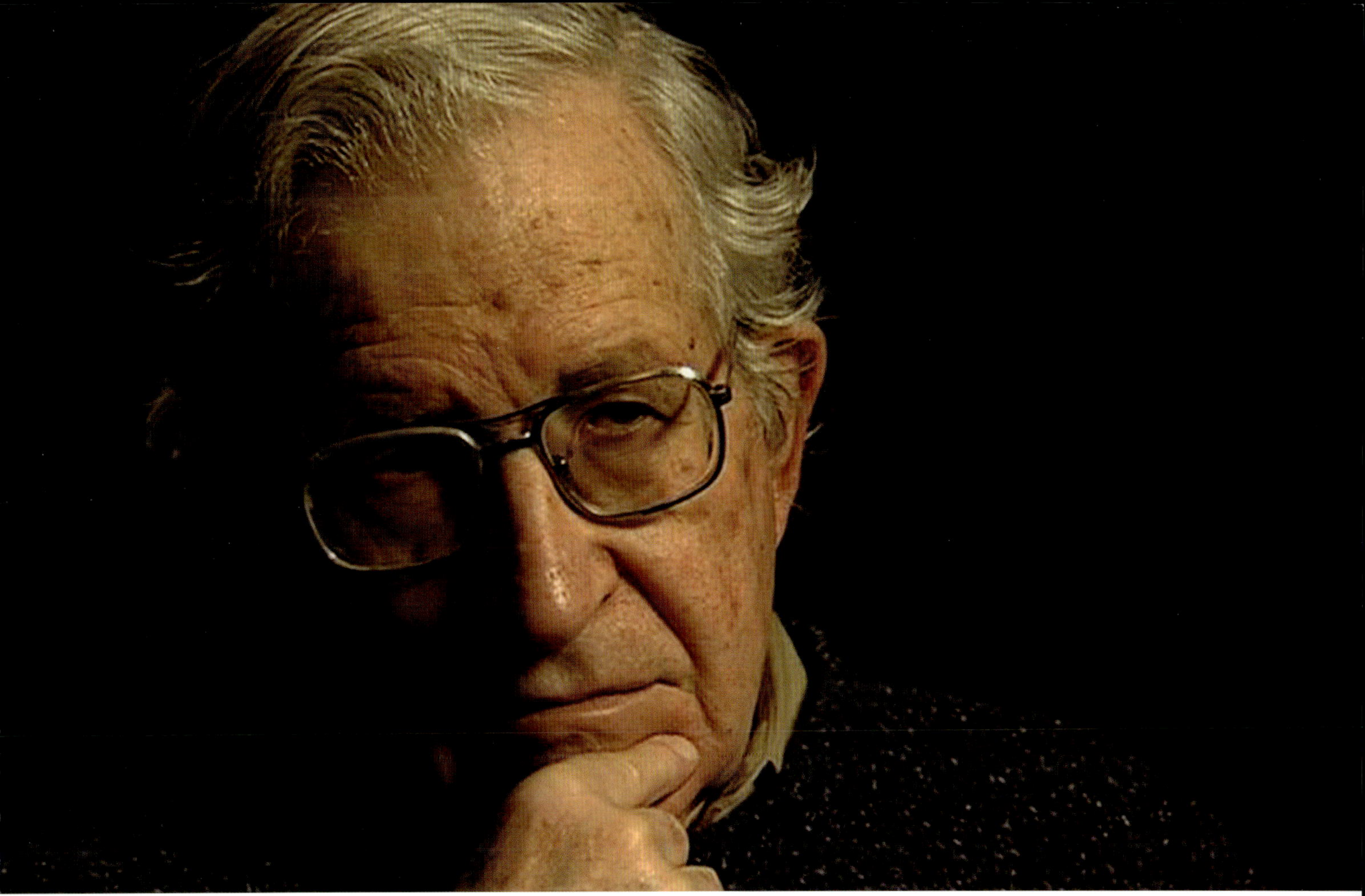

lifestyle – which has some attraction otherwise people wouldn't accept it... but it certainly doesn't have to be the one that's followed. I mean, I can give you personal stories about things like this, but... It requires a change.

And these changes can take place. The result of the 1960s – the activism of the 60s – did have a big effect on this, and it did make the societies much more civilized. That's one of the reasons that it's called 'the time of troubles'. It was making the countries too civilized. It's dangerous – and too democratic. But one of the effects was simply on lifestyle. So, during the late 1970s and the 1980s, you know, this was sort of reaching, becoming ingrained in large parts of the public. There was a very... and, you know, I don't know the figures for Europe, but in the United States there was a steady decline among younger people in use of tobacco, red meat, coffee, marijuana (which is less dangerous), but things that really are dangerous, just declined sharply. There was no legislation that said to not smoke tobacco, "don't eat red meat" – it was just a change in lifestyle; people wanted to be more healthy, more activity: go to the gym, jog, whatever it may be. Well, you know, these are changes in culture and lifestyle which, to some extent, separate people from the culture of consumption and distraction... By no means are they all like this. At the same time in the United States general health was declining. So, actually, height – which is a fairly good measure of health – is declining in the United States. The genes are pretty much all the same. But the tallest people are the Dutch or the Germans and not the Americans, they're shorter – you notice it when you go to the airport in Frankfurt and there are these six-foot tall women. It's just reflections of changes in lifestyle... probably even in hours of work. Hours of work have declined in Europe, gone up in the United States – and that has health effects. The things that they measure, say, GDP per capita, is going up less in Europe I suppose, because people are choosing a different lifestyle. They're choosing to have a couple of weeks off instead of copying a Japanese salary man who has to be taught what leisure is.

CP

NC There is a cultural fear that goes way back in American history, right from the beginning. You see it in popular literature and, in more recent times, in movies and television. It's been well studied. A kind of a constant theme in the popular culture has been that we're on the verge of destruction – somebody is about to destroy us – and, at the last minute, a super-hero comes, or great technologists invent a super-weapon, and it saves us. That's a theme that's run through for centuries.

A sub-theme is that the enemy that's going to destroy us is someone we're destroying. So, it's the native population that is going to come up wipe us out. Or it's the black slaves... they're just waiting for a chance to come and murder all the whites and rape the white women and so on. Or, later, it's the Chinese – you think they're here to run laundries but it's really those millions of Chinese that are coming in here and infiltrating, and they're going to take us over and destroy us. I mean, progressive writers like Jack London, a century ago, were writing that we have to destroy everyone in China by bacteriological warfare to prevent their insidious aim of doing this to us. Later... the Second World War – it was quite striking – it was the Huns, of course, and the Japs... But the Huns were treated (who were much more...as criminals, they were by degrees of magnitude, much worse) they were treated pretty calmly – this much I can remember – I mean, after all, they're blond and blue-eyed and white-skinned, they can't be that bad... The Japanese, on the other hand, were just vermin – they had to be crushed and wiped out and... You can read the public literature – "we have to wipe out their ant heaps" and they're "scurrying around like vermin" and so on and so forth. But they're going to destroy us unless we destroy them first, so we've got to destroy them.

And then, through the Cold War, you pick up one enemy after another: the Red Chinese, the Vietnamese, the Hispanic and narco traffickers, whatever they may be... Iran, today, is going to come and destroy us. How? Well, nobody's very clear – but somehow Iran will destroy us. Or maybe Cuba will destroy us. It can be the most minimal enemy. I mean, Ronald Reagan – who must be the most cowardly thug in history, now venerated after a huge PR campaign... In 1985,

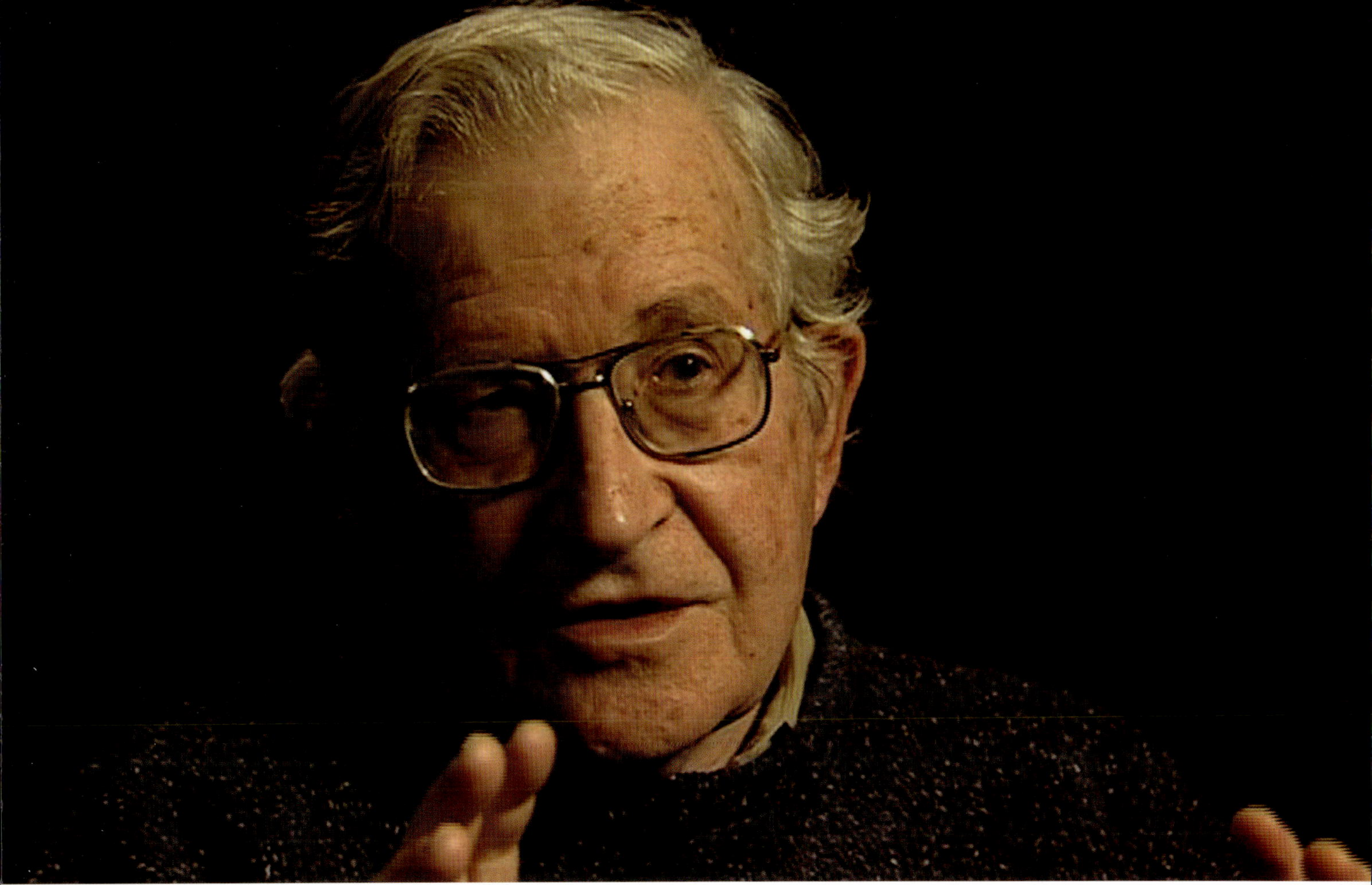

he declared a national emergency in the United States because of the threat to the security of the United States posed by the Government of Nicaragua, which had troops only two days away from HarlingenTexas. So, you know, Nicaragua's going to come any minute now and just overwhelm us. If you look at it from the outside, you don't know whether to laugh or cry. But this is a constant theme and it usually… it's sort of a steady sort of current – you know, which can always be stimulated when needed by cynical leaders with usual public relations techniques. When they decided they wanted to attack Iraq, they have Condoleezza Rice talking about the next time we hear from Saddam Hussein it'll be a mushroom cloud in New York – and everybody's terrified, and so on. And it can be whipped up into fear and paranoia, and it's very real.

It's an unfortunate feature of the culture – a strange culture in many ways – and part of it may be related to the fact that it's an extremely Fundamentalist society, and it's always been by far the most Fundamentalist country among the industrialized societies, maybe in the world. Two centuries ago, in the early days of the republic, there was a huge wave of Fundamentalist fanaticism about how we've got to quickly convert the whole world to speak English and save their souls… and the Second Coming, and so on. And it goes on and on like that. There's another one in the 1950s. There are several in the 19th – 20th Century. Right now, about a third of the population, probably, believes it doesn't matter what we do about global warming, say, because Jesus is coming – pretty soon, you know – and so if there's global warming, what's the difference? It's because God wants it – and He's coming soon, anyway, and those of us who are saved will rise to heaven and everyone else will be massacred – and it'll be wonderful.

In fact, when you look at even narrower positions like the incredible support for Israel, no matter what it does... and part of that is based on the fact that about a same third of the population, roughly, thinks we must support anything Israel does because that – in fact, even if it leads to, say, nuclear war – it's great, because that's how we read the book of Revelations, Armageddon, and so on and so forth, and then the Second Coming takes care of it all. There's a deep element of anti-Semitism in this because the Jews are all going to get massacred unless they convert. But the Jewish community and the State of Israel supports it – in fact, even has... missions to it because they like what they're getting in the short term, even if they all get wiped out after Armageddon. These are strong elements in the society. They're there in Europe, to a lesser extent – and there are other ones, that are worse, in Europe. But the propaganda – the State propaganda, the business propaganda – does play on these fears. I mean – take, say, Germany. Look, Germany in the 1920s/early 30s was the peak of Western civilization – the absolute peak – in the sciences, in the arts, literature...

... American political scientists regarded it as a model for democracy, and, within about three years, it was turned into a country of savage barbarians who'd carry out the worst crimes in history. And we're always right at the edge.

In fact, we're doing it right now and we don't notice it. Let's stick to the invasion if Iraq – and one of the first things that Rumsfeld, Cheney and Wolfowitz did was wipe out the origins of Western civilization: such as the Sumerian sites, the majority of them destroyed; the military base in Babylon; The National Museum, looted. You know – these are the riches of the origins of Western civilization. That's why the Iraqis regarded it just like the Mongol invasion. But it gets much worse. Yesterday, in the papers, you read that there was a suicide bomb in Mutanahbbi Street, which is important in Middle East culture. That was the centre of bookstores, literary cafés, and lively discussion in Iraq – which was in some respects the most advanced country in the Arab world. It survived right through the Saddam period... with debates, discussions – kind of like the Left Bank, you know, probably more advanced – but that's Mutanahbbi Street. Well, it was practically destroyed last year – but the final blow was the suicide bombing a couple of days' ago. Well, one of the newspapers quoted somebody there who, they say, in reverential tones repeated a well-known Arab proverb: Cairo writes, Beirut publishes, Iraq reads. OK – Iraq's not reading – we took care of that, from the Sumerians up to the present. But Cairo's still writing – so, if we can get out of our cocoons and become civilized, we can read with the writing in Cairo... which is, for example, that, during

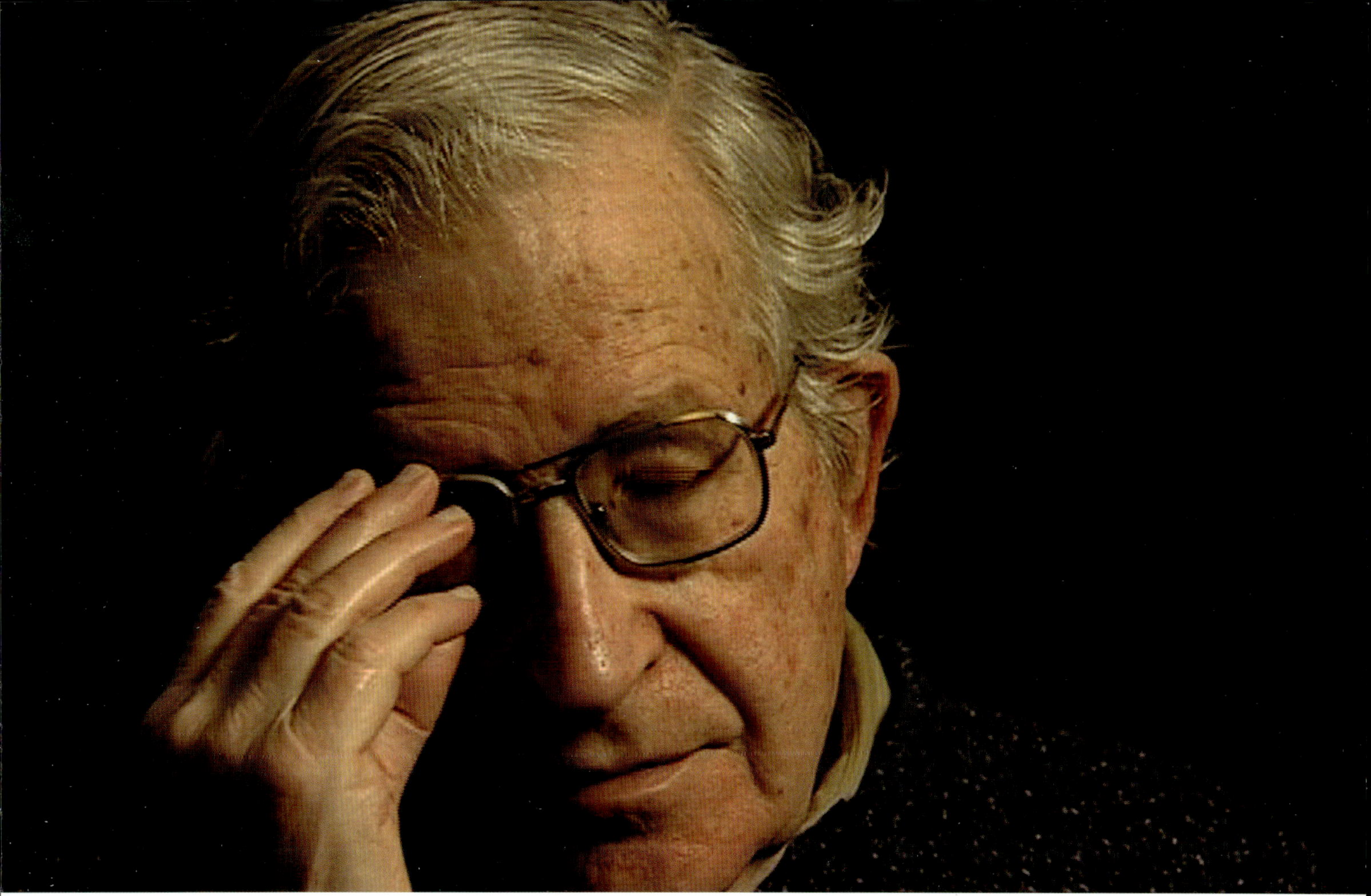

the US-Israeli bombing of Lebanon (which is US-Israeli – I say it because that's what it was), they specifically targeted the cultural areas in Beirut. They wiped out the centres of publishing; they wiped out some of the places where the bookstores are – because you must destroy the culture. We really are barbarians. We must destroy the cultures of the countries we are attacking. So now Cairo can still write but Beirut can't publish as much and Iraq can't read – and, just to make sure, we went all the way back to the Sumerians. Yes, it's a barbaric, savage culture that we live in. This doesn't mean anything in the West. OK, so we wipe out the history of Western civilization – modern culture, who cares? But it does mean something in other parts of the world, and we can't comprehend it... and then you ask, "Well, why do they hate us?" These are factors that have to be taken into account. We have to learn enough to understand what things mean to people in the world. Maybe we're too uncivilized to see them. It doesn't mean they don't.

List of Works

Embryo Firearms, 1995
Colt 45 guns in the earliest stage of production
19 x 13 x 2.4 cm (x2)
Collection of the artist. Special thanks to Colt Firearms Manufacturing, CT, USA

Shared Fate (Oliver), 1998
Doll cut in half by the guillotine that chopped off Marie Antoinette's head
42 x 20 x 10 cm
Collection of the artist

Stolen Thunder, 1997–98
Tarnish from famous peoples' silverware, collected on handkerchiefs
(selection from an ongoing series)
63 x 63 cm (x6)
Courtesy of the artist and Frith Street Gallery, London

Blue Shift, 2001
Lightbox containing the original nightgown worn by Mia Farrow in the 1968 Roman Polanski film 'Rosemary's Baby'
Collection of Jill and Peter Kraus

Blue Shift, 2002
Polaroids
8 x 8.5 cm (x4)
Courtesy of the artist and Frith Street Gallery, London

Subconscious of a Monument, 2002
Earth excavated from underneath the Leaning Tower of Pisa (to stop it falling)
Dimensions variable
Private collection, Turin, Italy

The Measure of a Man, 2004
Silver war medal drawn into wire
(from a series of 8 pieces)
61 x 61 cm
Collection of the artist

Shadow of a Doubt, 2004
Wood retrieved from a Texan ghost town, wire
306.5 x 144.5 x 62 cm
Courtesy of the artist and Frith Street Gallery, London

Heart of Darkness, 2004
Charcoal from a Florida Wildfire (prescribed forest burn that got out of control)
3.23 x 3.96 x 3.23 m
Courtesy of the artist and Frith Street Gallery, London

Measuring Niagara with a Teaspoon, 2005
Silver teaspoon drawn into a wire the height of Niagara Falls
(from a series of 7 pieces)
Wire drawing
63 x 63 cm
Collection of the artist

Endless Column III, 2006
Silver plated objects, crushed by 250-ton industrial press
426 x 41 x 2.5 cm
Courtesy of the artist and Frith Street Gallery, London

Measuring Liberty with a Dollar, 2007
Silver dollar drawn into a wire the height of the Statue of Liberty
(from a series of 7 pieces)
Wire drawing
63 x 63 cm
Collection of the artist

Bullet Drawings, 2007
Lead bullets drawn into wire
Dimensions variable (x9)
Courtesy of the artist and Frith Street Gallery, London

Pulled Tooth Drawing, 2007
Reclaimed dental gold drawn into wire
(from a series of 7 pieces)
63 x 63 cm
Courtesy of the artist and Frith Street Gallery, London

Chomskian Abstract, 2007
DVD
42 minutes
Courtesy of the artist and Frith Street Gallery, London
Commissioned by Ikon Gallery and Sharjah Biennial 8

Killing Time, 2007
DVD
19 minutes
Courtesy of the artist and Frith Street Gallery, London
Commissioned by Ikon Gallery and Sharjah Biennial 8

Brontëan Abstracts, 2006

Originally commissioned by the Brontë Parsonage Museum, Howarth

Deletions from the original manuscripts of Jane Eyre
Photographs
27 x 40.7 cm (x12)
Courtesy of the artist and Frith Street Gallery, London

Marks made in the margins by Emily Brontë
Photograph
31 x 34 cm (x4)
Courtesy of the artist and Frith Street Gallery, London

Emily Brontë's blotting paper
Photograph
40.6 x 38.1 cm
Courtesy of the artist and Frith Street Gallery, London

Charlotte Brontë's blotting paper
Photograph
48.3 x 38.7 cm
Courtesy of the artist and Frith Street Gallery, London

Emily Brontë's burnt comb
Photograph
34.3 x 40.6 cm
Courtesy of the artist and Frith Street Gallery, London

Anne Brontë's stained handkerchief
Photograph
38.1 x 27.9 cm
Courtesy of the artist and Frith Street Gallery, London

Charlotte Brontë's pincushion
Photograph
48.3 x 48.3 cm
Courtesy of the artist and Frith Street Gallery, London

Branwell Brontë's wallet
Photograph
41.3 x 48.3 cm
Courtesy of the artist and Frith Street Gallery, London

Charlotte, Anne & Emily Brontë's hair
Silver gelatin print of an SEM image
54 x 50 cm (x3)
Courtesy of the artist and Frith Street Gallery, London. With thanks to the Archaeology Dept. Bradford University

Emily Brontë's quill nib
Silver gelatin print of an SEM image
44.5 x 49.5 cm
Courtesy of the artist and Frith Street Gallery, London. With thanks to the Archaeology Department, Bradford University

Charlotte Brontë's quill pen
Silver gelatin print of an SEM image
30.5 x 30.5 cm
Courtesy of the artist and Frith Street Gallery, London. With thanks to the Archaeology Department, Bradford University

Charlotte Brontë's pen nib
Silver gelatin print of an SEM image
44.5 x 49.5 cm
Courtesy of the artist and Frith Street Gallery, London. With thanks to the Archaeology Department, Bradford University

Anne Brontë's needle
Silver gelatin print of an SEM image
44.5 x 49.5 cm
Courtesy of the artist and Frith Street Gallery, London. With thanks to the Archaeology Department, Bradford University

Pinhole made by Charlotte Brontë
Silver gelatin print of an SEM image
44.5 x 49.5 cm
Courtesy of the artist and Frith Street Gallery, London. With thanks to the Archaeology Department, Bradford University

Brontëan Abstract: Phyllis's Story
DVD
14 minutes
Courtesy of the artist and Frith Street Gallery, London

The Psychics
Fragments of a conversation between psychics Henrietta Llewellyn Davies, and Coral Temple (with questions asked by Cornelia Parker and writer Justine Picardie). Recorded at the Brontë Parsonage Museum August 2006
DVD
Courtesy of the artist and Frith Street Gallery, London

Biography

Lives and works in London

Solo exhibitions

2007
Never Endings, Ikon Gallery, Birmingham UK; MALI, Lima

2006
Bröntean Abstracts, Brönte Parsonage Museum, Haworth, West Yorkshire

2005
Focus: Cornelia Parker, The Modern Art Museum of Fort Worth, Fort Worth, Texas
New Work by Cornelia Parker, Yerba Buena Center for the Arts, San Francisco
Rorschach, Royal Institute of British Architects, London
D'Amelio Terras, New York
Perpetual Canon, Württembergischer Kunstverein Stuttgart, Germany

2004–05
Cornelia Parker: Installations from the Tate Collection, Norwich Castle Museum and Art Gallery, Norwich
Galeria Carles Tache, Barcelona, Spain
Finesilver Gallery, Project Space, San Antonio, Texas

2003
D'Amelio Terras
Guy Bartschi, Geneva
Galeria Carles Tache

2002
Frith Street Gallery

2001
GAM, Galleria Civica D'Arte Moderna, Turin, Italy

2000
Boston ICA, USA
Chicago Arts Club, USA
Aspen Museum of Art, USA
Philadelphia ICA, USA

1999
Frith Street Gallery, London
Avoided Object, Warburg Institute, London
Science Museum, London

1998
Serpentine Gallery, London
Mass: Colder Darker Matter , Deitch Projects, New York, USA

1997
ArtPace, San Antonio, Texas, USA
Casa Masaccio, San Giovanni Valdarno, Italy

1996
Avoided Object, Chapter Arts Centre, Cardiff

1995
(with Tilda Swinton) *The Maybe,* Serpentine Gallery, London
Gallery 102, Dusseldorf

1992
Eigen+Art, Leipzig
Vitrine Hortense Stael, Paris

1991
Cold Dark Matter. An Exploded View, Chisenhale Gallery, London
Vitrine Hortense Stael, Paris
Matter and What it Means, Spitalfields Heritage Centre, presented by the Whitechapel Gallery, London

1989
Matter and What it Means, Cornerhouse, Manchester UK

1988–89
Thirty Pieces of Silver, Ikon Gallery, Birmingham; Aspects Gallery, Portsmouth

1987
The Weather Within, Actualities, London

1980
Stoke City Art Gallery & Museum

Selected group exhibitions

2007
Projektion, Lenos Kunstmuseum, Linz
'Says the Junk in the Yard', Flowers East, London
8th Sharjah Biennial
Collective One, Galerie Guy Bärtschi, Geneva
Living in the Material World, National Art Center, Tokyo

2006–07
You'll Never Know, Hayward Gallery national touring exhibition, UK
The Shadow, Palazzo delle Papesse Centro Arte Contemporanea, Siena & Museo d'Arte Provincia di Nuoro, Italy

2006
Resonance, Firth Street Gallery, London
Thread, Ingleby Gallery, Edinburgh
Projektion, Museum of Art, Luzern
Cornelia Parker & Rob Smith, Royal Academy Schools Gallery, Hornsey, UK
Femme d'Europe, Saint Tropez

2005–07
Body: New Art from the UK, British Council touring exhibition
Water, Air, Earth, Ice. At the origins of life between Art and Science, Villa Croce Museum of Contemporary Art, Genoa
The Real Ideal, Sheffield Galleries, Sheffield, UK
Presence, Gimpel Fils, London
Bye-Bye blackboard…from Einstien and others, Museum of History of Science, Oxford, UK
Think & Wonder, Wonder & Think, Museum of Childhood, London
In the Neighborhood of Infinity, Sixteen:one Gallery, Santa Monica, USA

2004
The West Wing, St. Barts and The London Breast Cancer Centre, London
Speaking with Hands: Photographs from The Buhl Collection, Guggenheim Museum, New York
Other Times City Art Gallery, Prague
After Life, The Bowes Museum, County Durham, UK
The Disembodied Spirit, Contemporary Art in Kansas City
La Mort Devant Soi, Galerie Guy Bärtschi, Geneva

2003
Rancho Notorious Pearl, London
Knockabout, Spencer Brownstone Gallery, New York
Dust Memories, Swiss Institute-Contemporary Art, New York
Days like These, Tate Triennial, Tate Britain, London
Stacked, D'Amelio Terras, New York
The Disembodied Spirit, Bowdoin College Museum of Art, Brunswick, Maine
On tour: Contemporary Art in Kansas City and Austin Museum of Art
Independence, South London Gallery
Doublures, Musée Du Québec
From Dust to Dusk, Coppenhagen Udstillingsbygning

2002
To Eat or not to Eat, Centro de Arte de Salamanca, Spain
Continuitá: Arte in Toscana 1945–2000, Fattoria di Celle, Santomato di Pistoia, Italy
Summer Exhibition, Frith Street Gallery, London
Summer Palace, A Garden for Artists, Dusseldorf
Life is Beautiful, Laing Art Gallery, Newcastle UK
Pure Containment, Sculptures in the Collection, Arts Council of England, Orleans House Gallery, London

2001
Summer Exhibition, Frith Street Gallery, London
Solid State: Reflections upon the Real, Kettle's Yard, Cambridge
2000: the end of century. The seeds of the future Comune di Milano, Milan
The Silk Purse Procedure, Spike Island and Arnolfini Gallery, Bristol
Paper Assets British Museum, London

2000
British Art (part 1), Diehl Vorderwuelbecke, Berlin
Studio Stefania Miscetti, Rome
Between Cinema and a Hard Place, Tate Modern, London
Interventions, Milwaukee Art Museum, USA

1999–2000
1999 Drawings, Alexander and Bonin, New York

1999
Porcupines, 291 Gallery, London
Disaster, Harris Museum, Preston
Documents and Lies, Optica, A Centre For Contemporary Art, Montreal, Canada

Dards D'art, Mouches, Moustiques...Modernite, Arles Museum, France
0 to 60 in Ten Years, Frith Street Gallery, London
Melbourne 1st International Biennial, Melbourne, Australia
Postmark: An Abstract Effect, Site Santa Fe, USA
Violent Incident, Tate Gallery, Liverpool*Powder,* Aspen Museum of Art, USA
Appliance of Science, Frith Street Gallery, London
Avoiding Objects, Apex Art, New York

1998–99
Silver and Syrup: Selections from the History of Photography, Canon Photography Gallery at the V&A, Victoria & Albert Museum, London
Fun de Siecle: Irony, Parody and Humour in Contemporary Art, Walsall City Art Gallery and touring UK
Contemporary British Artists, Denver Art Museum, USA
Thinking Aloud, Kettle's Yard, Cambridge; Cornerhouse, Manchester; Camden Arts Centre, London

1997
Yoko Ono's Water Piece, Ormeau Bath Gallery, Belfast
Sarajevo 2000, Museum Moderner Kunst Stiftung Ludwig, Vienna
New Art from Britain, Kunstraum Innsbruck, Austria
Video / Projection / Film, Frith Street Gallery, London
Destroyer, Creator, John Weber Gallery, New York
Drawing Itself, The London Institute, London
Soon, Het Consortium, Amsterdam
Drawing Show, Glasgow Print Studio
The MGA Collection, The Fruitmarket Gallery, Edinburgh
Natural Science, Stills Gallery
The Turner Prize, Tate Gallery, London
Material Culture, Hayward Gallery, London
Night Shift, Schloss Pluschow, Germany
Building Site, Architectural Association, London
Critical Intervention, Jose Loff Gallery, Hartford Art School, USA

1996
Matter of Facts, Hawerkamp, Munster
City Space, Tivoli Gardens, Copenhagen
Some Drawings from London, 20 Princelet Street, London
Good News, Galerie 102, Dusseldorf

1995
Something The Matter: Helen Chadwick, Cathy de Monchaux, Cornelia Parker, Museo Municipal de Bellas Artes, Rosario, Argentina; Centro Cultural Recoleta, Buenos Aires; Museo Nacional de Bellas Artes, Rio de Janeiro; Galeria Athos Bulcao, Brasilia
A House in Time, Moderna Galerija Ljubljana, Slovinia
Eigen+Art, London
The Edge of Town, Jose Loff Gallery, Connecticut, USA
Five Artists, Frith Street Gallery, London

1994
XXII Bienal de São Paulo

1994–95
Art Unlimited, Royal Festival Hall, touring UK

1993–95
Recent British Sculpture, Hayward Gallery national touring exhibition, UK

1993
Eigen+Art, New York
Ha-Ha, Killerton Park, Devon
Topos, Grassimuseum, Liepzig

1992
Nigel Greenwood, London
Eigen+Art, Berlin
Whitechapel Open, London
Northern Adventures, Camden Arts Centre & St. Pancras Station, London
Through the Viewfinder, Stichting De Appel, Amsterdam

1991
Excavating the Present, Kettle's Yard, Cambridge
Tous Azimuts, Vitrine Hortense Stael, Paris

1990
The British Art Show, McLellan Galleries, Glasgow; Leeds City Art Gallery, Leeds; Hayward Gallery, London
Mostra, British School in Rome
Rome Scholars 1980–90, Royal College of Art, London
Edge 90, Newcastle, Glasgow
Whitechapel Open, Whitechapel Gallery, London
River, Goldsmiths, University of London
Drop, organised by Dean Clough, Halifax, touring UK
Systems of Support, Kettle's Yard, Cambridge

1986
Surveying the Scene, South Hill Park, Bracknell, Aspects Gallery, Portsmouth
National Garden Festival, Stoke-on-Trent
New British Sculpture, Air Gallery, London
No Place Like Home, Cornerhouse, Manchester

1985
Whitechapel Open, Whitechapel Gallery, London

1983
Sculpture by Women, Ikon Gallery, Birmingham
Ikon Touring Drawing Exhibition

1980
Midland View, Stoke City Art Gallery & Museum, touring

Awards, Commissions, Projects & Residencies

2006
Mood Train, off-site project, *Sicht Weisen*, Wuppertal, organised by Kunsthalle Dusseldorf

2005
For-site Residency, California

2004
Still Life with Reflection, installation, West Wing, Bart's Hospital, London

2003
Killing Time, sound piece for *Between the Ears*, BBC Radio 3

2001
Breathless, installation, British Galleries, Victoria & Albert Museum, London

2000
Meteorite Lands in Birmingham's Bullring, off-site project, Ikon Gallery, Birmingham, UK

1998–99
Artist's Residency, Science Museum, London

1998
International Association of Art Critics Prize (US), *Best Show by an Emerging Artist*, for *Mass: Colder Darker Matter*, Deitch Projects, New York

1997
Short-list nomination, Turner Prize, Tate Gallery, London
International Artist-in-Residence, ArtPace Foundation for Contemporary Art, San Antonio, Texas
Koopman Chair, Jose Loff Gallery, Hartford Art School, Connecticut
Brushes with fame, seven little frictions, sound piece, audio magazine, Audio Arts, London
Avoided Object, Artist's Insert, *Nature – International weekly journal of science,* Volume 389, Issues 6,648 – 6,652

1996
Meteorite Lands on Tivoli Gardens, off-site project, for *City Space*, European City of Culture event, Copenhagen

1995
Tate Christmas Tree, Tate Gallery, London

1992–95
Senior Fellow in Fine Art, Cardiff Institute

1992
From Here to Eternity, installation, Union Station, Los Angeles, organised by Wise/Taylor
Lost Volume: A Catalogue of Disasters, artist's book, Bookworks
Reading Matter, installation, Victoria & Albert Museum, London, organised by Bookworks

1991–92
Henry Moore Scholarship, Wimbledon School of Art, London

1990
Inhaled Roof, installation, *Edge 90*, Newcastle UK
Exhaled Schoolhouse, installation, *Edge 90*, Glasgow

1989
Artist's residency, British School at Rome Award
Left Luggage, installation, *Edge 90*, St Pancras Station, London

1988
Decanting Reservoirs, installation, St Peter's Church, organised by Kettle's Yard, Cambridge
Hanging Fire, installation, Forest of Dean, Gloucestershire

1986
Falling Façade, National Garden Festival, Stoke, UK
Stalactite City, installation, Siteworks Project, Southwark, London, organised by Bookworks

1980
Artist's Residency, Crewe & Alsager College, Cheshire

Collections

Arts Council of Great Britain
British Council
British Museum
Contemporary Arts Society
Deutsche Bank
De Young Museum, San Francisco
Fundacio La Caixa, Barcelona
Glaxo Wellcome Collection
Government Art Collection
Henry Moore Foundation
ICA Boston
Leicestershire Council
MAG Collection, UK
Milwaukee Arts Museum, Wisconsin
MOMA, New York
Museum of Modern Art , Fort Worth
Phoenix Art Museum
Tate Gallery
Victoria & Albert Museum, London
Yale Center for British Art, USA
Various Private Collections in Europe and the USA

Published on occasion of the exhibition
Cornelia Parker Never Endings

Ikon Gallery, Birmingham, UK
26 September – 18 November 2007

Museo de Arte de Lima
Lima, Peru
March – May 2008

Curated by Jonathan Watkins, assisted by Diana Stevenson

ISBN 978 1 904864 35 6

Ikon Gallery
1 Oozells Square, Brindleyplace, Birmingham, B1 2HS
t: +44 (0) 121 248 0708
f: +44 (0) 121 248 0709
http://www.ikon-gallery.co.uk
Registered charity no: 528892

Edited by Jonathan Watkins
Designed by Herman Lelie and Stefania Bonelli
Photography Alex Delfanne, Hugo Glendinning, Cornelia Parker, Norihiro Ueno, Steve White and Edward Woodman
Printed by Connekt Colour, uk

All images courtesy of the artist and Frith Street Gallery

Cover: *Brontëan Abstract (Charlotte Brontë's pincushion)* 2006 (detail)
Page 3: *Matt with 'Dynamite' in 1999* 2007

Distributed by Cornerhouse Publications
70 Oxford Street, Manchester, M1 5NH
publications@cornerhouse.org
t: +44 (0)161 200 1503
f: +44 (0)161 200 1504

Ikon gratefully acknowledges financial assistance from Arts Council England, West Midlands and Birmingham City Council.

ARTS COUNCIL ENGLAND
Birmingham City Council
The Henry Moore Foundation